DUKE ELLINGTON

His Life in Jazz

with 21 Activities

STEPHANIE STEIN CREASE

CHICAGO
REVIEW
PRESS

Library of Congress Cataloging-in-Publication Data

Stein Crease, Stephanie.

    Duke Ellington : his life in jazz with 21 activities / Stephanie Stein Crease. — 1st ed.

        p. cm.

    Includes bibliographical references, discography, filmography, and index.

    ISBN 978-1-55652-724-1

    1. Ellington, Duke, 1899-1974.   2. Jazz musicians—United States—Biography.

I. Title.

ML410.E44S75 2009

781.65092—dc22

[B]

2008023742

Cover and interior design: Monica Baziuk

Interior illustrations: Laura D'Argo

Cover images: Institute of Jazz Studies

© 2009 by Stephanie Stein Crease

All rights reserved

First edition

Published by Chicago Review Press, Incorporated

814 North Franklin Street

Chicago, Illinois 60610

ISBN 978-1-55652-724-1

Printed in the United States of America

5   4   3   2   1

To my dear family
and all in our world who go
"beyond category"
and hear the sounds of surprise.

CONTENTS

NOTE TO READERS

DURING DUKE ELLINGTON'S first years as a young professional musician in Washington, D.C., and then in New York City, he was sometimes a member of other people's bands, and also a bandleader himself. In those early years of Duke's career, his band went by several names, and was also given different names by club owners and reviewers. Some of those names include: The Duke and His Serenaders, The Serenaders, The Duke and His Kentucky Club Serenaders, The Washingtonians, Duke Ellington and His Cotton Club Orchestra, and Duke Ellington and His Famous Orchestra. The band also occasionally used pseudonyms to get around recording contracts. Don't let all the changing names confuse you. From the early 1930s on, the band was almost always known as Duke Ellington and His Orchestra.

ACKNOWLEDGMENTS

My sincere gratitude goes to my editor and publisher, Cynthia Sherry, whose insight and creativity helped shape this book. Also, very special thanks to my agent, Susan Ramer, developmental editor Lisa Reardon, designer Monica Baziuk, and the production staff at Chicago Review Press for helping see this project through to completion. I would like to especially thank Karen Oberlin Hajdu and Robert Crease for their encouraging comments as the manuscript progressed. I would also like to specially acknowledge James Herschorn, archivist at the Institute of Jazz Studies, Rutgers University, for his assistance with compiling most of the photos and artwork for this book. For additional photos and memorabilia, very special thanks to: David Hajdu; Morris Hodara, Corresponding Secretary of the Duke Ellington Society (TDES); and Che Williams, photo archivist, SONY/BMG.

Lastly, I would like to thank my son, Alexander Crease, whose joyful activities are an inspiration, as are those of India Schneider-Crease, my husband, Robert P. Crease, and my jazzy dog, Kendall.

INTRODUCTION

Exploring Duke Ellington's life (1899–1974) offers us a many-paned window to view the person, the artist, and his times and culture. Ellington's long career ran along its own track through a changing country and a changing world. His vast musical accomplishments include composing over 2,000 works, developing a unique style as a pianist, and maintaining one of the world's greatest jazz orchestras for over 50 years. His compositions molded a rich musical narrative from the sounds, colors, and textures of African American life: sometimes they took the form of pop songs, sometimes long orchestral works. Although his music always fell under the banner of jazz, Duke Ellington resisted musical categorizations of any kind. He once used the words "beyond category" as the highest compliment he could pay to another musician, and those words apply to him and his work, too. He was always reaching for something new and different in music.

Today, Duke Ellington's music keeps being discovered by people of all ages, everywhere. There are courses in music schools and conservatories devoted to his compositions, and annual international conferences about his music. His arrangements are studied and played by hundreds of high school jazz bands. You can hear his songs performed by young musicians—on piano, on violin, on trumpet, on saxophone—from grade school on up. Duke's music gives us inspiration to be creative on our own terms, in whatever we pursue. Whether it's a song like "It Don't Mean a Thing (If It Ain't Got That Swing)" or one of his Sacred Concerts, Duke's music is the work of an American master, telling an American musical story that touches people the world around.

TIME LINE

1877 Thomas Edison invents the wax-cylinder phonograph

1893 Chicago hosts World's Columbian Exposition

1899 April 29, Edward Kennedy "Duke" Ellington is born in Washington, D.C.

"Maple Leaf Rag" by Scott Joplin published as sheet music; sells over 100,000 copies

1901 Louis Armstrong born in New Orleans

The first flat-disk phonograph is introduced

1904 Ellington writes his first composition, "Soda Fountain Rag"

1915 United States enters World War I

1917 The Original Dixieland Jazz Band records the first 78-rpm jazz record, "Livery Stable Blues" (Side A) and "Tiger Rag" (Side B)

Ellington starts working with his first band, the Serenaders

Ellington marries Edna Thompson

1918 Race riots break out in 29 American cities

March 11, Duke and Edna's son Mercer is born in Washington, D.C.

1919 The 18th Amendment (also known as Prohibition) is ratified, outlawing the sale and manufacture of alcohol

1920 The 19th Amendment is ratified, guaranteeing women the right to vote

On election day, station KDKA in Pittsburgh makes the nation's first commercial broadcast announcing the presidential election results

Ellington moves to Harlem and becomes the leader of the Washingtonians

1923 Charles A. Lindbergh completes the first solo nonstop transatlantic flight

1927 Duke Ellington and His Orchestra become the house band at the Cotton Club in Harlem

1929 — Stock market crashes; the Great Depression begins

Ellington composes music for and appears in his first film, Black and Tan

1931 — Ellington's first hit record, "Mood Indigo," sells over one million copies

1933 — Duke Ellington and His Orchestra go on their first tour of Europe

1936 — Franklin Delano Roosevelt reelected president

The height of the swing and big band era

1941 — December 7, Japanese attack Pearl Harbor; the United States enters World War II

1943 — Duke Ellington and His Orchestra makes their debut at Carnegie Hall

1945 — First atomic bombs dropped on Hiroshima and Nagasaki, Japan; World War II ends

1950 — Television becomes affordable for American families

1954 — The Supreme Court rules in Brown v. Board of Education that racial segregation in public schools is unconstitutional

1956 — Duke Ellington and His Orchestra triumph at the Newport Jazz Festival

1957 — Duke Ellington meets Queen Elizabeth in Great Britain

1963 — Duke Ellington and His Orchestra go on their first tour of the Mideast, sponsored by the U.S. State Department

1964 — The U.S. Civil Rights Act is passed

1965 — Ellington presents the first of his Sacred Concerts in San Francisco

1968 — Dr. Martin Luther King Jr. is assassinated

1969 — Astronaut Neil Armstrong is the first person to walk on the moon

Ellington is awarded the Presidential Medal of Freedom

1974 — May 24, Edward Kennedy "Duke" Ellington dies in New York City

1999 — Centennial of Ellington's birth is celebrated worldwide

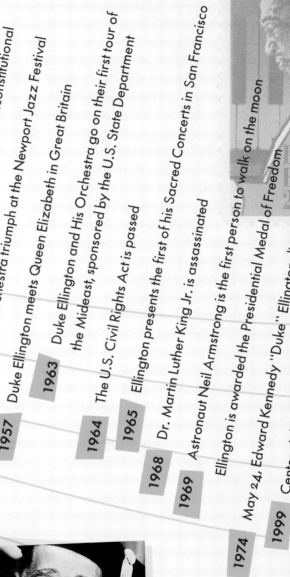

Duke Ellington
New York City
22¢ USA

1

CATCHING A TUNE

"There have been so many extraordinary and inexplicable circumstances in my life. I have always seemed to encounter the right people, the right place at the right time, and doing the right thing to give me the kind of instruction and guidance I needed."

—DUKE ELLINGTON

Do you know anyone whose skill or talent suddenly took you by surprise? Like your best friend from elementary school. He was funny and liked to have a good time, but he never got terrific grades or stood out at sports or anything. And the next thing you knew, there he was at 15, playing the piano and being a big hit at parties, and even making some money at it. And to top it off, he was a really good piano player!

Well, that was true of Edward Kennedy "Duke" Ellington, who did not show much interest or talent in music as a child. Yet years later, he became one of the greatest jazz composers and bandleaders who ever lived.

Edward Kennedy Ellington was born April 29, 1899, in Washington, D.C. He was the second child of James Edward and Daisy Ellington. Edward's younger sister, Ruth, wasn't born until he was 16, so he was mostly raised as an only child (the Ellingtons' first child died as a baby). He was never at a loss for playmates,

My mother—the greatest—
and the prettiest
My father—just handsome—
but the wittiest
My grand-daddy
natural born proud
Grandma so gentle—and so fine

(FROM "MY MOTHER, MY FATHER," MY PEOPLE, DUKE ELLINGTON, 1963)

Publicity photo of Duke Ellington, then a young bandleader and pianist. Courtesy David Hajdu

2

though. Young Edward had a large extended family of cousins to play with, and aunts and uncles who visited constantly. They lived in a tight-knit middle class African American community in the northwest section of Washington, D.C., known as the "Uptown District." Ellington often said how lucky he was to grow up there and to be raised by parents whose complete confidence in him helped him on his road to success.

Ellington's parents were both 20 years old when he was born. His mother, Daisy, was very loving and watched over her new baby constantly. She was still getting over the death of her first baby and so fretted over Edward's every sneeze. Edward grew up surrounded by Daisy's sisters and aunts, who all treated him like a little prince. His mother called him blessed so often that he was convinced he was indeed blessed, and that only good things would come to him.

Edward's childhood was far more comfortable than that of his own father. James Edward Ellington was born in 1879 in rural North Carolina to a family of ex-slaves. When James was a teenager, he and his family moved north to Washington, D.C., along with many other African American families who settled there in the years after the Civil War. They were all looking for jobs and better living conditions. James, who only had an eighth-grade education, quickly learned how to get along in the city. He started out as a coachman and driver, and worked for various people, including a wealthy doctor named Middleton Cuthbart.

James was smart and responsible. By the time he and Daisy married, he was the doctor's butler and ran the whole household. According to Ruth, Edward's younger sister, James educated himself by reading his way around Dr. Cuthbart's library, "from the floor to the ceiling, all four walls." James also worked as a caterer for other families, and at several special events that took place at the White House.

In contrast to her husband's Deep South background, Daisy Kennedy Ellington came from a well-established middle class family in Washington, D.C. and completed high school. Her father was a policeman, a respected profession for a black man early in the 20th century. Daisy was beautiful and dignified. She was a thoughtful and spiritual person, and always looked for ways to inspire her son. She often told Edward that all races were equal and that the world held much promise for him—there was nothing that he could not achieve.

James Ellington made enough money so that his family could live in a big, comfortable house in the Uptown District. This neighborhood was less than two miles from the White House, in the northwest section of Washington, D.C., which was then a segregated city.

Through his work, James became an expert about fine foods and wine, silverware, and crystal, and wanted to provide the best things he could for his family. As Edward later wrote, "J.E. always acted as though he had money, whether he had it or not. He spent and lived like a man who had money, and he raised his family as though he were a millionaire."

One of the Ellington family's prized possessions was their piano. In the early 1900s, the piano was the heart of the home and was the family's entertainment center. Both of Edward's parents played the piano, and relatives and friends frequently gathered around to sing and entertain each other. James played by ear and worked out popular songs of the time, and Daisy could read music. She loved to play hymns, and also taught herself some of the latest ragtime favorites. Edward clearly enjoyed music, and joined in singing around his family's piano and in church. As he got older, he liked hearing the ragtime pianists who played at soda fountains and cafés and other spots around his neighborhood.

Edward's childhood coincided with the exciting first years of a new century, and the syncopated sounds of ragtime. Ragtime music was the rage in those years, in the days before the word "jazz" was even in use as a musical style. Ragtime was the rock 'n' roll of the early 1900s, enjoyed and performed by young people, black and white, for dances and parties and as parlor music. Ragtime originated in the café district of St. Louis, Missouri. There, in the city's honky-tonks and social clubs like the Maple Leaf Café, the best pianists (the so-called Piano Professors) such as Scott Joplin and Tom Turpin refined their musical style and showed off their original compositions.

Ragtime music is syncopated, which means that the accents are on the weak beats of a musical measure, not the strong beats. Syncopation is what made the ragtime style sound new and different. The catchy melodies and

HOME ENTERTAINMENT—THE PIANO

The grand piano was invented in 1702 by an Italian craftsman named Bartolomeo Cristofori for a member of the wealthy Medici family of Florence. By 1726, Cristofori had perfected the piano's striking hammer action, which produced a stronger and more rounded sound than its predecessor, the harpsichord. Well into the 1800s, the piano was a luxury item for the aristocracy, but by the late 1800s, affordable upright pianos became available. Owning a piano was a sign of a family's respectability, and playing the piano was a special skill for girls, in particular, to have, in an era when parents helped their daughters find suitable husbands. More than that, pianos were everywhere, in schools, hotels, drugstores, and restaurants, and good pianists were called upon for all kinds of occasions, whether they played classical music or ragtime.

rhythms of ragtime pieces like Joplin's "Maple Leaf Rag" were popularized by traveling pianists and musicians in vaudeville shows and revues. Long before electronic music technology—CD players or iPods—existed, pianists helped spread this new music from town to town and neighborhood to neighborhood. Pretty soon, ragtime music was everywhere. Sheet music editions of Joplin's ragtime compositions and those of other ragtime composers were big sellers, and in the early 1900s, ragtime music was arranged for marching bands and early dance bands.

Edward loved music, but there was another new American pastime he loved even more—baseball. American League Park, home of the Washington Senators and one of the earliest professional ballparks, was not far from Edward's neighborhood. Excitement about the nearby games and the Senators were part of his childhood and that of his friends, who played pickup games almost every day.

Then one day, when Edward was seven, wham! He got hit accidentally with a baseball bat while his mother happened to be watching him play. On the spot, she decided that sports were too dangerous and that piano lessons would be better for him. Always wanting to please his mother, Edward went along with this plan, but he was not really interested in his lessons and frequently skipped them.

SCOTT JOPLIN—
THE KING OF RAGTIME

Scott Joplin was born in 1868 in the northeastern part of Texas, and spent his early years on a farm where his father, an ex-slave, was a laborer. In 1880, the family moved to the small town of Texarkana, and music was a big part of their life: his mother played the banjo, and his father taught violin to Scott and two of his brothers. Scott also took formal lessons on piano, and his teacher inspired him to compose music. Joplin left home as a teenager to make his living as a traveling pianist. Sometimes, he joined his brothers' minstrel show, performing songs and skits in small towns in the Southwest.

When Scott was 20, he settled in Sedalia, Missouri, and it was there that his career as a composer truly began. Joplin's ragtime compositions, formally written-out pieces for piano, were very popular in Sedalia's gambling dens and dance halls. In 1899, he played his "Maple Leaf Rag" for a local music publisher; it was one of the first ragtime compositions published and became a sheet music bestseller. Joplin published many other successful ragtime tunes, too, including "The Entertainer."

In 1911, Joplin moved to New York, where ragtime was the rage. By then, he had fallen out with his publisher and was ill, but he struggled to keep working. He wanted people to appreciate the richness of ragtime music: he wrote larger compositions, including a ballet and an opera that used ragtime themes and rhythms. He produced his opera, *Treemonisha*, bringing ragtime to the concert stage for the first time. Joplin himself predicted that his music would achieve far greater recognition after his lifetime, and that is exactly what happened. "The Entertainer" won an Oscar in 1973 for best song in a motion picture, and Joplin was awarded a posthumous Pulitzer Prize for *Treemonisha* in 1976, honoring his contributions to American music.

Baseball was Edward's true interest in elementary school, and getting hit with a bat did nothing to keep him from the game. He loved baseball so much that he got a job selling peanuts and drinks at the ballpark so he could watch the professional games as often as possible.

All in all, Edward had a happy childhood. The Uptown District where he lived was a big part of it. It had been a close-knit black community for decades, with an atmosphere of racial pride that was reflected in its schools, churches, theaters, businesses, and civic organizations. "U" Street, the lively main street in the neighborhood, was lined with cafés, restaurants, and theaters owned by African Americans. Dunbar High School, the first public high school for blacks in America, was a college preparatory school. Howard University, founded in 1867, was the first black university in the country and attracted many African American teachers and scholars to the city. When Edward was growing up, Washington, D.C. had the largest black population in the United States (approximately 87,000 people) and was an exciting place for African American writers, artists, and intellectuals to live, just as Harlem would become in the 1920s.

Even so, Washington, D.C. was also full of racial contrasts. The city legalized segregation in 1896. "Jim Crow" laws put segregation into practice. Neighborhoods were strictly racially segregated. There were separate schools for African American children and white children, and public facilities all had separate entrances. Before 1896, almost 10 percent of government jobs in Washington, D.C. were held by African Americans; afterward, those jobs were not offered to blacks, and the most commonly held jobs were as domestic help or in service professions. Sadly, there was discrimination even within the African American community. Lighter-skin people did not mix socially with those who had darker skin, and the many uneducated rural people who moved to the city did not always find the opportunities they hoped for.

Edward's family and community were an oasis from the harsh realities of racism and the segregated stores and restaurants downtown. In many ways, Edward's childhood was that of a typical American boy of the time: he loved sports, spending time with his friends, fishing, and finding adventures in the woods and fields near his neighborhood. He also spent a lot of time drawing and painting, and his parents encouraged his early interest in art, as well as everything else he did.

Ellington's life story does not have the "rags-to-riches" drama of the jazz trumpet legend Louis Armstrong's, whose rise from extreme

Illustrate a Sheet Music Cover

FROM THE LATE 1800s through the 1930s, sheet music publishing was a huge and profitable industry, and the attractive cover designs, printed in color, boosted sales for many songs. A good design conveyed a lot of information about the music: whether it was happy or sad, romantic or playful. Here is an example of a cover design for a Duke Ellington song from 1931. Notice how the designer was aiming for something "jazzy," including the type style for the song title. Try your hand at designing a sheet music cover.

YOU'LL NEED
- ♪ Recording of a favorite song
- ♪ CD, cassette player, iPod, or other music listening device
- ♪ Scratch paper
- ♪ Pencils
- ♪ 9 x 12-inch sheet of sketchbook paper
- ♪ Felt-tip markers or poster paint
- ♪ Computer (optional)
- ♪ Glue

Listen to a recording of your favorite song, or pick out a song that you would like to create a sheet music cover for. It could be a popular song or one of Duke Ellington's many hit songs that are still performed today, such as "Sophisticated Lady," "Take the 'A' Train," or "Mood Indigo."

Listen carefully to the song a few times, and see what images pop into your mind.

Do the lyrics tell a story, or express a mood? Does the song make you think of a special place? Let your imagination settle on a particular image that you think expresses something about the music. Then, make a pencil sketch. Your design should include the song title in large lettering, and the names of the composer (the person who wrote the music) and the lyricist (the person who made up the song's words) in smaller lettering. You can usually find their names on the back of the CD case or in the CD booklet; this information comes up automatically for music downloads. Invent your own decorative lettering style or print one from your computer. Once you are happy with your sketch, make a final version on the 9 x 12-inch paper, and color in your design with felt-tip markers or paint. If you like, you can create parts of your design (such as the title) on a computer; print those parts out and glue them on to your final design.

The sheet music cover for "Mood Indigo," one of Ellington's first hit songs.
Institute of Jazz Studies

7

poverty to international fame is a real-life Cinderella story. But Duke Ellington's life and career were full of surprises. The biggest surprise of all was that Ellington was a late bloomer in music. Both he and his parents thought he was going to be an artist—not a musician. He gave up on piano lessons pretty quickly and, though he liked music, he didn't seem very interested in pursuing it. After finishing middle school, Edward was going to attend Armstrong Manual Training School for high school, so that he could major in commercial art.

TURNING POINTS

The summer of 1913 marked a turning point for 14-year-old Edward Ellington. For one thing, that was when he got his nickname. One of his best friends started calling him "Duke" as a joke and a backhanded compliment. They were both good-looking boys who liked trendy clothes, were smart and funny, and thought of themselves as cool. Pretty soon everyone started calling Edward "Duke"—and the name stuck.

That summer was also a turning point for Duke musically. Suddenly he was captivated by the popular music he heard around his neighborhood. He went to listen to the piano players that seemed to be everywhere—at drugstores and soda fountains, restaurants, and even the neighborhood pool hall that he and his friends liked to sneak into. Duke started playing the piano again, trying to copy the songs and styles of the pianists he heard.

That same summer, Duke and his mother went to Asbury Park, a resort town on the New Jersey shore, to get away from the heat of Washington, D.C. Duke got a job washing dishes at a small hotel, and all he and his coworkers talked about was music. Someone told him about a young ragtime pianist named Harvey Brooks, who lived in Philadelphia. On his way back to Washington, Duke stopped off in Philadelphia and went to look him up.

Harvey Brooks was probably about 16 or 17 when Duke met him, and was already working as a musician. Duke was impressed by everything about him. Harvey was flashy, his clothes were sharp, and he even wrote his own music. He was generous about showing Duke piano techniques to play the ragtime style, especially how to coordinate the syncopated parts for the left and right hand. Duke wrote about their meeting: "He was swinging, and he had a tremendous left hand, and when I got home I had a real yearning to play. I hadn't been able to get off the ground before, but after hearing him I said to myself, 'Man, you're just going to *have* to do it!'"

Activity
Create a Ragtime Rhythm

SYNCOPATED RHYTHM or syncopation made ragtime sound new and different. Syncopation occurs when the accented notes shift from the "strong beats" (the first and third beats of a measure) to the "weak beats" (the second and fourth). A measure marks off the number of beats of music for a certain tempo (fast or slow). Most ragtime pieces were composed in 2/4 time: there are two whole beats per each measure, which are ≠ up into quarter notes, eighth notes, and sixteenth notes. The syncopated beats (one *two* three *four*) played against a steady rhythm in the bass notes created the "raggedy" sounding rhythm. This activity will help you explore and play a ragtime rhythm.

YOU'LL NEED
♪ A recording of Scott Joplin's "Maple Leaf Rag" or "The Entertainer" (you can hear Joplin's piano roll version at this link: http://music.minnesota.publicradio.org/features/9905_ragtime)
♪ CD player, computer, iPod, or other music listening device
♪ Pencil
♪ Music paper or plain paper

Listen carefully to "Maple Leaf Rag" or "The Entertainer." Tap your foot to the steady beat of the bass notes (on beats one and three). Now try tapping to the accented second and fourth beats. If you are doing this with a friend, you can tap one part and your friend can tap the other.

The musical examples at right show what these beats look like in rhythmic notation. Tap out Rhythm A on a table. Did you notice which beat the accent falls on? It is on the first beat of each measure (the downbeat). Now tap out Rhythm B, which has the accents on the

second and fourth beats, and even on the second of a pair of eighth notes (the upbeats). Now play rhythm C, which combines the two. Does it remind you of the rhythm of "Maple Leaf Rag"?

Make up a two-measure or four-measure pattern of your own. You can use music paper, or copy the musical staff on a sheet of plain paper. Then tap out your own rhythm, alone or with a friend. Does it sound syncopated?

Duke at the piano; publicity photo from the late 1920s. Institute of Jazz Studies

That was it. When Duke returned home, he started practicing the piano for hours at a stretch. Baseball no longer seemed very important. He sought out and listened to the best ragtime pianists in Washington, D.C. The way these pianists looked—their clothes and their stage manners—caught Duke's attention as much as their music. Duke started to work hard at copying whatever they did, even their eye-catching hand gestures. Local pianists such as Doc Perry, Claude Hopkins, Louis Brown, and Gertie Wells were skilled musicians who could read music and play any style, including classical. Doc Perry, in particular, was generous with his time, and showed Duke the latest tunes and how to achieve certain effects and patterns. He was happy to have such an enthusiastic student.

Yet even as a teenager, Duke could not read music very well. He trained himself to learn tunes by ear and trust his memory. He learned to do what the professionals did, which was to memorize new songs almost instantly, so that he could practice them at home. That's what the musicians called "catching a tune."

The spread of ragtime music went along with a new craze for popular dancing that ragtime inspired. Duke and his friends couldn't help but notice that the girls they knew really liked this trend. As soon as Duke could play well enough to fake his way through some songs, his friends convinced him to play the piano at a party.

Duke immediately became the center of attention. He was a hit with the dancers and the girls and enjoyed all the newfound attention. But his repertoire was still pretty limited. He needed to come up with a lot of new songs to play to get through another party like this first one. While practicing at home, he started trying to modify the tunes he knew so that they seemed like different compositions, and learned the art of "faking it."

"From then on," Duke wrote years later, "I was invited to many parties, where I learned that when you were playing piano there was always a pretty girl standing at the bass end of the piano. I ain't been no athlete since. But if at that time I had ever thought I was learning the piano to make a living, I would never have made it!" ∞

Having fun with musical instruments, early 1930s. Institute of Jazz Studies

2

THE DUKE AND HIS SERENADERS

"Do I believe I was blessed? Of course I do! In the first place, my mother told me so, many, many times, and when she did it was always quietly, confidently. She was very soft-spoken, and I knew that anything she told me was true. . . . So until this day I really don't have any fears, beyond what I might do to hurt or offend someone else."

—Duke Ellington

Duke Ellington's biggest gift from his mother and father was his confidence. His mother in particular had complete faith that he would succeed in anything he chose to do. Both of his parents wanted him to get a good education so that he could nourish his talents and make a living on his own terms. The African American community he was raised in, the Uptown neighborhood, helped nurture this in its children.

Additionally, Duke got a firsthand education from his father about presenting himself well, being a self-starter, and providing a good life for his family. James Ellington was charming, witty, articulate, and always well-dressed. James started his own catering business and used his employer's social connections to get extra work for himself and his friends at the special events hosted by Washington's well-to-do families. This kind of networking was a great model for Duke, one that he would put to use in his early career as a bandleader. Duke was devoted to his mother, and even revered her. But in terms of his personality, Duke was more like his father: extremely outgoing, witty, and charming, especially to women.

As Duke spent more and more of his time involved with music, by the end of his junior year of high school, he was no longer sure what would be the better professional direction for him—commercial art or music. People asked him to play at parties more and more frequently and at the soda fountain where he worked part-time. Now, music had become a driving force for him. But sometimes his involvement with music led him to do irresponsible things. He cut classes to play the piano in the school gymnasium, or skipped out of school to go listen to local piano players and seek them out for lessons and advice.

Duke gives a cheerful helping hand, early 1930s.
Institute of Jazz Studies

DUKE'S PIANO PARENTS

Doc Perry was one of the most popular pianists and black bandleaders in Washington, D.C. when Duke was a teenager. Perry was a versatile, skilled pianist who could play classical music and ragtime, still the most popular style of the time. A review in the Uptown newspaper, the *Washington Bee*, described a performance in 1917: "Doc Perry's Society Band played the latest dance music and a local artist sang popular songs through a megaphone while beautifully gowned young women tangoed with their well-groomed partners."

Duke knew he needed to learn more material and more musical skills if he was going to get paying musical jobs, or even just to play for parties with his friends. He started going over to Perry's house twice a week for lessons. Perry helped Duke finally learn how to read music, an important skill for playing with a band, and how to play the songs of the day in a syncopated ragtime style. Perry must have been impressed with Duke's ability and his persistence, and didn't charge him at all. He became Duke's main musical mentor during this period. Duke wrote: "He was my piano parent and nothing was too good for me to try."

Soon, Perry started asking the young pianist to occasionally substitute for him at Wednesday afternoon tea dances, so Perry could go to his higher-paying job at a hotel lounge. Perry also helped Duke develop a professional attitude: to dress appropriately and be polite and reliable, qualities that Duke was already nurturing in himself.

Duke still did not know a lot of songs, nor could he read music very well. But he needed

MUSIC TECHNOLOGY— PIANO ROLLS AND THE PHONOGRAPH

In the late 1800s, two path-breaking inventions helped people enjoy music in their homes, whether they had musical skills or not.

One of them was a self-playing piano, or player piano (often confused with the trade name, the Pianola). The instrument used cylindrical paper "piano rolls" with tiny holes that represented the musical notes; the player mechanism was powered by suction, and activated by two foot pedals. The operator could change the speed of the music, and how loud the notes were, without playing any of the notes by hand—and still look like a good pianist. Coin-operated versions of these player pianos started showing up in theaters, cafés, and drugstores in the form of nickelodeons. Some piano rolls were "cut" by the greatest classical pianists of the day, as well as by the ragtime composer Scott Joplin, and the great stride pianists James P. Johnson and Fats Waller.

In the early 1900s, the Victor Talking Machine Company started manufacturing affordable record players (gramophones), giving rise to a new industry, music recording. By the 1920s, the record player replaced the piano and the player piano as America's first choice in home entertainment. The latest trends in popular music—jazz, the blues, and even early country "hillbilly" music—went hand in hand with the booming recording industry.

new material to perform. One afternoon around 1914 or 1915, while working at his soda fountain job, he was suddenly asked to substitute for the regular piano player, who was too drunk to play! Duke took over, but ran out of songs after about 45 minutes, so on the spot he cobbled together a piece from fragments of songs he knew. That night, he went home and worked on it and gave it the working title "Soda Fountain Rag" (later he renamed it "Poodle Dog Rag"). It was based on popular songs of the day, mixed with flashy arpeggios (rolled-out chords) and runs that Duke could easily play. Though it was a reinvention of familiar songs, it sounded original and new.

Later in his career, Duke Ellington would become skilled at being a practical composer—tailoring a tune for an occasion or coming up with new material quickly. At this point, though, Duke didn't really spend that much time composing. The only other piece that Duke composed as a teenager that has survived is a blues number that was a big hit among his teenage friends. "What You Gonna Do When the Bed Breaks Down?" was a slow dance tune, what Duke and his friends called a "hugging-crawl" tune—in other words, just right for "dirty dancing."

As Duke began to play more frequently in public, he kept looking out for the best piano players to listen to and observe. Louis N. Brown was one of them; he could play any kind of musical style, from popular tunes to classical pieces. Another was Louis Thomas, a popular bandleader and conductor who founded the Capital City Clef Club. This was a professional musical organization for black musicians in Washington, D.C., modeled on the New York Clef Club, which was founded in 1910 by James Reese Europe, a pioneering African American bandleader, composer, and arranger.

Duke was confident about performing in public, even though he needed more skills and experience. Soon, other piano players started asking him to substitute for them, too. Through all this, Duke was still a high school student. Would you find it surprising that his grades were not very good? Music often kept him out late at night, and he missed classes during the day. Still, he excelled in his art classes.

In the fall of 1916, Duke's senior year in high school, he entered a poster contest sponsored by the National Association for the Advancement of Colored People (NAACP), America's oldest civil rights organization, which was founded in 1909. Duke won first prize, a scholarship to Pratt Institute, a famous art school located in Brooklyn, New York.

Duke's dilemma—whether to concentrate on art or music as a profession—intensified. The scholarship was a great opportunity. But

Think Like a Composer—Write Your Own Blues

THE BLUES DEVELOPED from work songs of slaves and their descendants. Many important blues musicians came from the Mississippi Delta and other parts of the South. As huge numbers of African Americans moved to northern cities after World War I, the country blues became the city blues. The blues can be happy or sad, fast or slow. The blues can be sung, or performed as an instrumental tune. Jazz big bands like Duke's often played some blues arrangements.

Most blues songs have a few things in common: the use of blue notes (or bent notes), and the 12-bar blues form. Blue notes are notes that fall between regular musical intervals in a scale; these are usually the third note of the scale and the seventh. The "12-bar" blues is a 12-measure form divided into three four-measure segments. These segments typically use three chords based on three notes of the scale: the first note, the fourth, and the fifth; the chords are called the I-chord, the IV-chord, and the V-chord. This activity is based on Duke Ellington's "C-Jam Blues," a 12-bar blues, with a melody that has only two notes. The jazz singer Ella Fitzgerald made up lyrics to this tune that basically just said: "Hey, let's go down to Duke's place." Try writing a 12-bar blues like this one, or try writing your own blues lyrics.

YOU'LL NEED

- ♪ Recording of Duke Ellington's "C-Jam Blues." You can find this on a CD of *Duke Ellington's Greatest Hits,* or on *Ella Fitzgerald Sings the Duke Ellington Songbook*
- ♪ CD player, computer, iPod, or other music listening device
- ♪ Pencil
- ♪ Music paper

Listen to "C-Jam Blues." Do you notice that the melody really has only two notes? Then, see if you can count off the 12-bar blues pattern, and listen for the I-IV-V-I chords. Now, either make up your own 2-note blues melody or write your own blues lyrics to "C-Jam Blues." The lyrics can be about your pet, your house, or anything in your life.

For example:

Can I, can I have some ice cream?
Give me, give me lots of ice cream.
If I don't get some then I will go scream.

I don't want no squash or sweet peas.
I don't want no squash or sweet peas.
Give me, give me lots of ice cream . . .

Repeats three times

Ba by   let's go down to   Dukes place

The melody stays the same for the whole 12-bar blues sequence:

[I]			
F⁷	F⁷	F⁷	F⁷
[IV]		**[I]**	
Bb⁷	Bb	F⁷	F⁷
[V]		**[I]**	
C⁷	C⁷	F⁷	F⁷

Activity
Design a Concert Poster

AFTER DUKE LEFT high school, he kept up his art skills by painting signs and posters, and even formed a sign-painting business with a friend. They made signs for small neighborhood businesses, and also made posters for dances and concerts. The best music posters combine words and images to quickly convey a band's image and what kind of music they will be playing (rock, jazz, classical). A good design is—above all—attention grabbing. Try your hand at creating an eye-catching poster for a concert.

YOU'LL NEED

♪ A recording by your favorite band
♪ CD player, computer, iPod, or other music listening device
♪ Scrap paper
♪ Pencil
♪ Computer and printer (optional)
♪ 20 x 28-inch sheet of poster board, or large sheet of white sketchbook paper
♪ Colored markers or poster paint

Pick out a band or musician that you really like and want to get other people excited about hearing at a concert (it could be a "pretend" concert near your neighborhood). While you are doing this activity, listen to their music. On a piece of scrap paper, write out all the information about the concert: the name of the group or musician, a theme ("World Tour"), and the date, time, and location of the concert. Include any special information, such as "One Night Only!" or "First West Coast Appearance!"

Try a couple of sketches on scrap paper, showing the entire design: images plus words. Envision how everything will look on the big poster board. You can create an abstract design with wild colors and shapes, if it suits the music. Or you can draw the band. Once you've decided on the image, you can design your own lettering to fit the image; or, type the letters on a blank document on your computer and play around with various font sizes and styles.

Now transfer your final idea onto the poster board, blocking in your lettering by hand or gluing a printout from your computer to the board. Neatly apply color with paint or markers. A good poster will make you and your friends want to take action—like going to the concert!

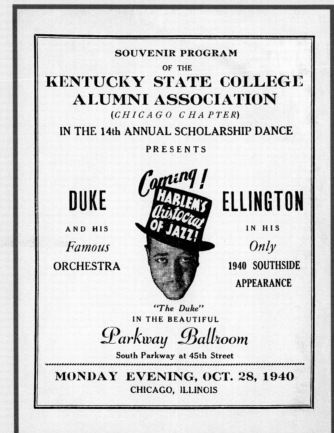

Poster for a dance in Chicago.
Institute of Jazz Studies

18

Duke was already earning some money as a piano player, and he was attracted to the world of entertainment. He turned the scholarship down. Duke was sure that he could make a good living with music, just like his "piano parents" were able to do. He not only turned down the scholarship, he dropped out of high school three months before graduation.

DUKE TURNS PROFESSIONAL

Many of you might be scratching your heads by now. What kind of role model is Duke Ellington, anyway? A high school dropout? A ladies' man? Today, leaving high school would be considered a tragedy and an absolute mistake with a capital "M"! But times were very different then. Duke and many other teenagers didn't finish high school because they were expected to start working and earning money as soon as they could, and most young people didn't go to college.

Duke was a risk taker and ambitious. After he left high school in the spring of 1917, he concentrated on finding more work, both as a musician and as a commercial artist. He started getting more jobs with dance bands, mostly as a substitute for other musicians. He put his commercial art training to use, too, and found work painting signs and posters. Duke was en-

ergetic, optimistic, and well liked. Everything he did led him to believe he would succeed.

Substituting for other pianists was not always so easy for Duke, especially playing with dance bands. Though Duke's reputation around Washington had grown to that of a "decent piano player," his sight-reading skills were still not very good, and most dance bands used printed parts. A new or substitute musician was expected to be able to read his or her part on the spot and keep up with the band. Once, when Duke was trying to "fake" his way through reading the piano part, he overheard other musicians say he wasn't playing the "correct chords." Sometimes, Duke misjudged social situations, or who the audience would be. Doc Perry once got mad at him for showing up at a special event at the British Embassy wearing clothes that were flashy and trendy instead of formal.

These kinds of experiences didn't discourage Duke, and through them he learned what being a professional musician meant. One of the most important things he learned was what a bandleader actually did. The bandleader was the business contact for getting gigs. He had to make sure his musicians got to the job on time and dressed properly for the occasion, and he made sure that the band got paid. The bandleader was also responsible for musical decisions: how big the band would be (depending on the budget), what style and what pieces would be performed, and what the musical arrangements would be. So the bandleader typically took a higher fee than his band members, who were called "sidemen."

After being involved in the dance-band scene for a few months, Duke decided that he could be a bandleader, too. He started playing at parties with a band he called The Duke and His Serenaders. The group was made up of a few friends who played instruments, most of whom were better musically trained than Duke was. There were the three Miller brothers (all around Duke's age), who were sons of a local music teacher and bandleader: they played guitar, saxophone, and drums. The youngest members of the band were 13-year-old Otto "Toby" Hardwick, who could play string bass and saxophone, and 12-year-old Arthur Whetsel, who played trumpet and cornet. Duke sometimes added other musicians, too, and the band became bigger or smaller depending on the occasion (and whether Toby and Arthur's parents allowed them out that night). Sterling Conway played banjo and joined them for some jobs; his brother Ewell was Duke's partner in the sign-painting business.

"The Duke's Serenaders" was the name that would stick for a few years, as would a couple of the musicians. Arthur Whetsel and Toby Hardwick would stay with Duke for the next few years, through his rise to stardom.

One of the Serenaders' first jobs was at True Reformer's Hall. The four-story building was a landmark in Duke's neighborhood, used mostly for community events. It was designed, built, and paid for by the African American community, which was a big undertaking for all the people who brought that project to completion. The hall housed a huge auditorium, as well as smaller rooms upstairs where high school students often held their own parties and dances. Ellington vividly recalled the first time he played there: "I played my first date at the True Reformer's Hall on the worst piano in the world. I played from 8:00 P.M. to 1:00 A.M. and for 75 cents. Man, I snatched that money and ran like a thief. My mother was so proud of me."

Rex Stewart, who would join Ellington's band in the 1930s as a trumpet player, went to some of the dance parties at True Reformer's Hall. He said that Duke and the Serenaders were so popular at the Hall that he was crowned the "King of Room 10."

Meanwhile, shortly after Duke left high school, America was in the midst of radical change. In April 1917, the United States declared war on Germany and officially entered World War I. Washington, D.C. quickly became a hub for military personnel, officers

Activity
Make a Washtub Bass

DUKE'S SERENADERS PLAYED on typical dance-band instruments. But in cities like New Orleans and Washington, D.C., there were also plenty of street musicians who used homemade instruments, like jugs, washtub basses, and banjos made from boxes and string. These "jug" bands or "skiffle" bands played popular songs, the blues, and ragtime tunes, punctuated by the thump of a washtub bass or tapped-out rhythms on a corrugated metal washboard. Try your hand at making a small washtub bass.

Adult supervision required

YOU'LL NEED

- ♪ Large metal mixing bowl or pot or large coffee can
- ♪ Heavy nail
- ♪ 2 eye screws
- ♪ Hammer
- ♪ 6-foot nylon string or fishing line
- ♪ 3-foot-long, ½-inch-diameter dowel

1. Turn the bowl or pot upside down, and hammer the nail into the metal to make a hole.

2. Hammer a small hole into both ends of the dowel, so it will be easy to attach the eye screws in steps 3 and 4.

3. Turn the bowl or pot on its side, and attach the dowel to the eye screw, so the eye (loop) of the eye screw will be underneath, and the screw goes into the end of the dowel. You will then be able to pivot the dowel.

4. Screw the other eye screw to the top of the dowel, so the eye (loop) is at the top of the dowel.

5. Run string or fishing line from the top of the dowel to the bottom, tying it off through the hole on the bottom eye screw.

See how many different notes you can get by placing your fingers on different parts of the string against the dowel, which shortens or lengthens the string. Can you play something that sounds like a scale? You should be able to get a range of notes. You can also experiment with what kinds of sound you get from applying different pressure on the string, or tipping the bowl, and hearing how the sound resonates off the metal bowl.

and soldiers, coming and going. Young men in their early 20s were required to register for service, and many African Americans joined the armed forces.

Duke turned 18 on April 29, 1917. He became a messenger for the War and Navy Department, and his father got a job drawing blueprints for the navy. Almost all of Washington, D.C. was involved with the war effort, and the country's capital was bristling with activity and military people on the move.

For Duke, the war also meant more musical jobs. Washington was such a hub of activity that there was a continuous round of social events and dances—for farewells and home-comings, and to boost morale. During 1918 and 1919, Duke worked with his own group almost every night of the week. He also acted as a musical contractor, which means he got jobs for a few other bands and kept a percentage of their fees for himself.

Duke was earning good money in those days—sometimes as much as $150 a week—and got professional training that went beyond the musical. He started learning how to play the right kind of music to fit different occasions, and even how to find new clients. He got a telephone, which was still rare for most households. Duke had an interest in new technology of any kind, whether it was music-related, such as the gramophone, or the telephone and automobile. He immediately realized how the telephone could advance his career as a bandleader: he was now easy to reach, and the phone book was a great way to advertise his band. Years later, he wrote: "In those days whenever anyone wanted anything in Washington, D.C., they looked in the phone book. . . . There were a lot of war workers in town; they were all strangers who didn't know Louis Thomas from Duke Ellington or anybody else. When they wanted a party, they'd look in there and see who played music and call up."

Duke's advertisements paid off. These were significant years for popular culture in America despite a war going on in Europe and many Americans serving abroad in the armed services. The dance craze led to more steady work for musicians, who had to tailor their music for what the dancers wanted—danceable smooth rhythms and interesting arrangements. In fact, dance fever helped pave the way for a new style of music played by bigger and bigger bands that could get a ballroom full of people energized. That new style was called jazz.

In July 1917, the first jazz record was made by the Original Dixieland Jazz Band, and caused a sensation. The two songs the band recorded were a complete novelty: "Tiger Rag" and "Livery Stable Blues" showed off one kind of early jazz style from New Orleans. Theirs was a rough style with a snappy rhythm and wild improvising, which means the musicians played freely with the melodies of these songs. This was sometimes called "jazzin' the tune." Other New Orleans musicians, like Louis Armstrong, the clarinetist Sydney Bechet, and pianist Jelly Roll Morton, had a more elegant way of playing, even though their music was just as rhythmic and spirited.

Then and now, the word "jazz" is used to describe the playing of very different musicians. Even so, a distinct jazz dance-band style developed during World War I and throughout the 1920s. Ellington and other dance-band musicians latched onto a syncopated rhythm that was less choppy than ragtime rhythm. Bandleaders also came up with musical arrangements that had specific parts for the different instruments; the musicians might have written-out (notated) parts, or might work out their parts with the band and memorize them. Musical arrangements showed off the properties of the instruments, especially the different brass and woodwinds, and helped the band form a unified sound. The arrangements included space for a featured soloist to improvise. The new jazz style had roots in ragtime and the blues.

By the early 1920s, the word "jazz" was more commonly used, though for many people it was still associated with music from bars and street life. It was a name for music that your parents might not want you to listen to. But meanwhile, respectable dance bands in Washington, D.C. and other cities started calling themselves jazz orchestras, and sheet music was classified as "jazz" or "jass." The word "jazz" had become a buzzword in black Washington.

"Jazz is based on the sound of our native heritage. It is an American idiom with African roots . . ."

DUKE GROWS UP

As for Duke's personal life, he had quickly become an adult—perhaps too quickly! On July 2, 1918, Duke married a girl from the neighborhood, Edna Thompson, who had become his sweetheart. Edna had attended Dunbar High School and played the piano, too. They soon moved into their own house, a few blocks away from both sets of parents, and

THE NEW ORLEANS JAZZ PIONEERS

Many early jazz musicians came from New Orleans, a musical melting pot with influences from Europe, Africa, and the Caribbean that were the legacy of the slave trade. New Orleans was a nonstop musical city with many social clubs, parades, and picnics where musicians could show off their virtuosity (technical expertise and musical skills).

Buddy Bolden (1877–1931) is considered the first-ever jazz trumpeter, and the first of the New Orleans trumpet kings. He was a great improviser, who could play very high notes with ease. By 1900, "King" Bolden was in demand all over the city, in saloons and dance halls as well as high-society functions, and every young trumpet player wanted to follow in his footsteps. Sadly, when he was only 23 years old he started suffering from alcoholism and mental health problems and spent the last half of his life in a mental institution.

Jelly Roll Morton (1890–1941), a pianist, composer, arranger, and bandleader, was one of the most colorful New Orleans musicians of all. He claimed to be the "inventor of jazz," and was playing piano in New Orleans honky-tonks when he was 12. He became a traveling musician until he settled in Chicago in the 1920s, a city where many New Orleans musicians moved for better-paying jobs. It was in Chicago that Morton formed his groundbreaking group the Red Hot Peppers, and his arrangements made the band a stand-out.

Sydney Bechet (1897–1959) was the king of the clarinet and soprano saxophone. He grew up around the great New Orleans trumpet kings, and soon played with all of them. He left New Orleans for Chicago in 1917, joined the orchestra of Will Marion Cook, and went to New York and Europe. Bechet and Ellington crossed paths in New York City in the late 1920s, and Bechet added his whirling sound to Duke's band.

Louis Armstrong (1901–1971), one of America's first African American celebrities, spent his first years living in a shack with his mother. When he was 12, he was sent to the Colored Waif's Home for Boys because he was caught shooting a gun into the air on New Year's Day. He learned to play trumpet in the home's marching band, and four years later was one of the stars of the New Orleans music scene. In the 1920s Armstrong became a main attraction in Chicago nightclubs. He then moved to New Yourk City, where he became a star. Armstrong's strong high notes were legendary, and his gifts as an improviser have made him a lasting musical influence.

Louis Armstrong, already a jazz star on trumpet, c. 1927. Institute of Jazz Studies

their son Mercer was born on March 11, 1919. (A year later, a second pregnancy ended in the baby's death.)

Duke was almost 20 years old when his son was born. He claimed to be making about $200 a week, which was a lot of money in those days. He worked hard for his money. He was busy performing with his own group and contracting out jobs for other bands. He sometimes worked as a part-time messenger for the navy, a job he did during World War I. At the same time he had a small sign-painting business: he painted signs and designed posters, and even painted backdrops for the Howard Theater.

With all these activities, Duke could support his own family and help his parents out, too. He liked to provide well for everyone, just like his father had. He also enjoyed modern conveniences. He bought a car, which made getting from one job to another easier and faster. He bought a small house for his family, and one nearby for his parents. He was a clever businessman and used every opportunity to get more work. For instance, if you went to him to get a sign painted for a dance, he'd suggest you hire his band for the music. Or if you came to him to hire a band, he'd ask you who was painting your sign.

Around this time, Duke was also getting more work for his bands outside the black community. He and his band played at fancy balls in Virginia during the racing and hunting seasons, and they performed at dances and parties for Washington's elite. "All the embassies and big shots in Washington were hiring small bands to play at parties," he said. "It didn't seem to make much difference *what* band—they just hired *a* band." The Serenaders also played at cabarets, pool halls, and nightspots where brawls broke out and they had to run for it.

> **"To me, jazz means simply freedom of musical speech!"**

In later years, Duke would always give credit for his success to his family and his Uptown neighborhood upbringing, where young people were always encouraged to do their best at whatever path they chose. But things were not always peaceful in his hometown. During the summer of 1919, race riots erupted in several cities, including Washington, D.C., Chicago, Detroit, and Atlanta. James Weldon Johnson, a leading black writer who lived in Harlem, called it "Red Summer" because of all the bloodshed. Ellington never spoke or wrote of this, nor did he ever mention any incidents involving his family or friends.

Duke Ellington during the Jazz Age.
Institute of Jazz Studies

More than anything else, Duke was dedicated to his work as a bandleader. Even then, the dance-band world was competitive, and he knew that he had to keep improving his own musical skills and the overall sound of the band. He started taking music lessons from Henry Grant, a musician, music educator, and composer who was then director of the Washington Conservatory, a prestigious music school for African American students. Grant, like Doc Perry, became a mentor for Duke. A founder and director of several musical groups, Grant personified the rich diversity of black Washington's musical world—its classical musicians, glee clubs, and church choirs. Grant believed that standards of excellence could apply to popular music, too, and found Duke to be an eager student. He continued to work with Duke to improve his sight-reading, and also taught him about harmony, theory, and composition.

Many years later, Grant's daughter remembered Duke Ellington coming to their house twice a week for lessons. She said: "I think he just wanted to be a little more knowledgeable about music, and Papa was right there for him. . . . Duke could stand out on the porch and talk with us until my father was ready for him. . . . You couldn't forget him. Our porch became quite a popular place and all the girls around wanted to come to look at him."

As the new decade, the 1920s, approached, there was a nonstop demand for dance music in Washington. The Duke's Serenaders were definitely "at the right place at the right time," and Duke continued to be successful as a musical contractor as well. Much of his success was due to being a clever businessperson, someone who was able to put his love of music to work for him. No one was calling him a musical genius, yet! Duke was entranced by the sounds of the new style—jazz. This captivating, rhythmic, bluesy music seemed to echo the sense of freedom and independence that young Americans were experiencing. The Jazz Age was born, and it would nourish Duke's musical ambition. In October 1919, Duke Ellington placed a new advertisement in the Washington, D.C. phone book:

IRRESISTABLE JASS
Furnished to our Select Patrons

THE DUKE'S SERENADERS
Colored Syncopators

E.K. Ellington, Mgr.

3

THE SERENADERS BECOME THE WASHINGTONIANS

As Duke entered his 20s, the "Jazz Age" of the Roaring Twenties began. The Jazz Age took place in a country racing toward modernity. World War I was over, the economy was booming, and the sounds of cars, trolleys, and trains filled city streets. Popular culture and music echoed this optimism with a newfound stylishness and snappy rhythms. But this culture thrived during the age of Prohibition; the outlawing of liquor in 1920 fostered an underground scene full of crime, corruption, gambling, and bootlegging—all of which was part of the Jazz Age, too.

Jazz was still kind of a dirty word, even in Ellington's circle. But whatever one called the music that Duke and his friends were playing, Washington, D.C. in 1921 was the right place and the right time for dance music. There were many dance halls, and there was a dance somewhere every night.

One of the features at these halls was the battle of the bands, the forerunner of *American Idol* or TV talent contests. These band contests were a big attraction. For the musicians, the sense of friendly rivalry sharpened everyone's performance style. Musicians also learned new tunes at these events. The weekly band battles at the Howard Theater were a particular favorite for musicians and audiences alike. The bands that performed ranged in size from 3 instruments to 30, and the musicians had all ranges of expertise. The winner was declared by popular vote from the audience, and which band got the loudest and longest applause.

Jazz music was still controversial; the music was looked down upon by all kinds of people, black and white. Just as today, when many parents and teachers are offended by rap lyrics and "dirty dancing," the latest jazz music and dances that teens liked were frowned upon, even by Ellington's parents. The newspapers were full of stories: "Does Jazz Put the Sin in Syncopation?"; "Does Jazz Cause Crime?"

But jazz had taken root. The new music echoed everything about the new America. It was modern-sounding and fast-paced. It also had a new element that sounded really uninhibited: improvisation. Through their improvised solos, jazz musicians showed off both their musical and technical skill—by playing really high notes, or really fast runs, all in the context of the tune itself. The free and spontaneous quality of the music appealed to audiences and especially to young people, who, for the first time, were exerting a force on culture.

The Howard Theater was a showcase for the best black entertainers and bands, but Washington had many other places to hear bands and go dancing. Favorite spots for black audiences were the Capital City Clef Club and the Dreamland Café, or Murray's Casino, a huge dance hall that held 1,800 people. The Duke's Serenaders played at just about all of these places, and took part in many of the band battles. Duke and his musicians played their part to the hilt; they looked sharp, spoke well, devised attention-grabbing routines, and made sure they'd be hired for the next job. By playing together so often, their musical skills grew and they sounded like a real unit, a solid band. They attracted the attention of other young musicians who came to town. One of them was Sonny Greer, a drummer

Activity
Learn to Improvise

IMPROVISATION IS A key ingredient in jazz. There are many ways that jazz musicians come up with ideas for their improvisations. A musician can ornament the original melody, or improvise a variation based on the melody so that it is still recognizable; that means adding extra notes or altering the phrases. Jazz musicians also improvise when inspired by rhythm. They alter melodies so that accents fall in completely different places, or they repeat notes or displace them; this is called a rhythmic variation. Improvisers also respond to one another, so at times jazz improvisation is like a conversation. This activity explores jazz improvising by listening to Duke's "C-Jam Blues" again. Then, you can try improvising to a simple tune like "Jingle Bells."

YOU'LL NEED
♪ Recording of Duke Ellington's "C-Jam Blues"
♪ CD player, computer, iPod, or other music listening device
♪ Tape recorder (optional)

Listen to "C-Jam Blues" (we first heard this tune in chapter 2), and hear how the band members enter one by one to play the simple melody together. Then, listen to the first improvisation or "solo" played by Ray Nance on violin (he also played trumpet in Duke's band). This is his time to improvise. Then, trumpet player Rex Stewart uses completely different ideas for his "solo." Three other musicians play short solos next, before the band repeats the melody together and ends the tune.

Now try improvising yourself, or with a friend. Look at the musical example of "Jingle Bells" at right. Sing the melody once. Now sing Example A, a melodic variation; then try Example B, a rhythmic

variation. See if you can sing one part and have your friend sing the other at the same time. Do you end up finishing at the same time? Do your notes sound harmonious? Can you still recognize the melody? What other ways might you improvise on this tune?

"Jingle Bells"

Example A: Melodic Variation

Example B: Rhythmic Variation

Sonny Greer, Duke Ellington's famous drummer. Institute of Jazz Studies

who had come down to Washington for a visit and ended up working in the orchestra of the Howard Theater, a good, steady job for a musician.

Sonny was 20 years old, like Duke, and from New Jersey. He had been working as a drummer since he was 15, with various groups who performed in the resort towns on the New Jersey shore, and even in New York City. He immediately attracted attention for his trendy clothes and for his showmanship. "Sonny Greer was sensational," said saxophonist Otto Hardwick. "He was our first contact from New York, and he was quite flashy and everyone took a liking to him." On stage, Greer did a lot of tricks with his sticks and cymbals and was also an excellent drummer. Elmer Snowden was another talented young musician who showed up in Washington, D.C. around the same time as Greer, in 1920. With a flair for playing ragtime and jazzy rhythms on the banjo, he quickly became the number-one banjo player in town.

Pretty soon, both Sonny and Elmer were playing with Duke's Serenaders, and Duke and his friends wanted to hear about their experiences working in other cities. Sonny was the resident New York expert; he had many tales of the city because he had two aunts who lived there, who he often stayed with. Years later he admitted, "I painted a glowing picture, a fabulous picture. We stood around drinking corn and telling lies, and I won the lying contest." Greer made New York City and Harlem sound like the Land of Oz.

Duke's ears perked up for these stories, and also for the music of the famous New York musicians who came to play at the Howard Theater. He particularly liked seeing the well-dressed bands that were so well-rehearsed; many of the musicians played more than one instrument—switching from clarinet to saxophone with flair.

Duke's closest brush with fame at this time was with James P. Johnson, an important jazz pianist who came to Washington in November 1921 to perform at the Convention Center. Johnson's specialty was stride piano, a New York style that was even more impressive than ragtime piano. Just a few months before Johnson's visit, Ellington had spent many hours perfecting Johnson's most famous piano piece, "Carolina Shout." Duke learned it by slowing down a player-piano roll and copying the notes. "Carolina Shout" quickly became a showpiece for Duke. His friends persuaded him to play it in front of Johnson, who was so impressed he then invited the younger musicians to show him around D.C.'s nightspots.

Duke's night out with Johnson, and Sonny Greer's tales of New York City fired up Duke's imagination. Bit by bit, Duke was hearing New York City calling.

In March 1923, Duke got an opportunity to go to New York. A bandleader named Wilbur Sweatman contacted Sonny Greer about joining his band for a week's work at the Lafayette Theater in Harlem. Sweatman was a clarinetist and bandleader who'd been famous on the traveling vaudeville show circuit for years. Sweatman's band accompanied vaudeville variety acts like dancers and magicians, and

THE JAZZ AGE

During the Jazz Age, urban America was flourishing along with the new skyscrapers. All kinds of people were on the move: immigrant families and the Great Migration of thousands of African American families to northern cities. Young Americans from all over the country moved to cities for better jobs and opportunities.

Young urbanites and flapper girls partied to the sounds of hot jazz. The flapper girl, with her short hair, short dresses, and independent attitude, was an early feminist, daring society to tell her how to dress, think, or act. On the serious side, women got the right to vote in 1920, and were seeking to gain a foothold in all the professions.

Jazz music was the right soundtrack for the time, and its popularity spread due to technology: the radio. The first commercial radio station began broadcasting in 1919, and by the end of the 1920s there were radios in more than 10 million households, bringing the latest musical trends right into your home.

THAT'S ENTERTAINMENT!—
MINSTREL SHOWS AND VAUDEVILLE

Can you imagine a future world with no TV or movies? Amazingly, the two most popular forms of American entertainment of the 1800s, minstrel shows and vaudeville, don't exist anymore and are unfamiliar terms to many people.

Minstrel shows—small traveling shows with comedy skits and music—have a clouded history, despite their widespread popularity from the 1840s through the 1870s. Much of their entertainment value was built on racial stereotypes: white actors in blackface performed skits poking fun at the "Negro of plantation society," and then at the uneducated slave-turned-sharecropper. The popularity of these shows gave rise to all-black troupes whose actors also wore blackface and played up these same caricatures. By the early 1900s, ragtime and blues musicians and dancers performed in these shows.

The minstrel shows evolved into bigger, more structured vaudeville variety shows, performed in theaters across the country, a step up from saloons and tents. Almost every town and city had its theater "palace," and the vaudeville shows, black and white, were designed to present something for everyone.

A typical vaudeville show offered a little bit of everything in 8 to 14 acts: magicians, musical numbers, dance numbers, acrobats, jugglers, comedy routines, and rare appearances by unusual celebrities of the day—like Helen Keller! Vaudeville's appeal was that everyone could afford a ticket; you didn't have to be educated or cultured—you just came to have fun. The vaudeville stage opened its arms to everyone—African Americans, immigrants, and female stars. The same stars that made it in vaudeville—comedians such as Bob Hope and the Marx Brothers, and great tap dancers like Bojangles Robinson and the Nicholas Brothers—would soon become stars of the new media—radio and "talking pictures," which helped put vaudeville out of business.

his claim to fame was being able to play three clarinets at once. Sweatman was also one of the first black musicians to take part in a recording session. Greer accepted Sweatman's offer but insisted that the leader hire Duke and their friend, the saxophonist Otto Hardwick, too.

Sweatman's current band was one of several acts in an all-star vaudeville show. Sweatman agreed to take on Sonny, Otto, and Duke to complete his six-piece band of banjo, drums, bass, sax, clarinet, and piano. This was Ellington's first experience in a vaudeville show. He and his friends worked long hours for their money. A typical week started on Monday and ran through the following Sunday. They played a show every night, and a matinee every day. They also played a midnight show on Friday and continuous shows on Sunday.

Even though Duke, Sonny, and Otto were busy performing, they were thrilled to be in New York City, and especially in Harlem, at the northern end of the city. It seemed like a dream come true. In the early 1920s, Harlem had the largest concentration of African Americans in the country, with almost 100,000 black residents within 25 square blocks; by 1930, that grew to 165,000. People moved there not just from the South but from all over the country and the Caribbean. Every street held an adventure.

Harlem's nightlife was already legendary, but Harlem also became home to many African American writers, social thinkers, and intellectuals, bringing about the literary movement known as the Harlem Renaissance.

REACHING FOR THE BIG APPLE

Duke, Sonny, and Otto were so excited about being in New York that they passed up Sweatman's invitation to keep working with him on the vaudeville circuit. They decided to try their luck in New York City on their own. This turned out to be much harder than they had thought it would be. The New York music scene was just as competitive then as it is today. They tried to find musical work through their few contacts, but nothing came of their efforts. Sonny Greer made a little money during the day winning games of pool; he shared whatever he won with Duke and Otto, and they slept at the homes of his relatives. Duke, always well-dressed and charming, managed to meet some of the leading pianists in Harlem, including another star of stride piano, Willie "The Lion" Smith. Duke tagged along after Smith to speakeasies and cafés, so he could watch and learn from the older musician, just like he had with Doc Perry in Washington, D.C. Duke also followed Willie to Saturday night rent parties. In the 1920s, many people threw these parties at their homes to help them raise the money they needed to pay the rent. The hosts often sold decorated tickets a few days ahead of time, and word spread. It was easy for Duke to find out who would be playing at a Saturday night party.

The Harlem Renaissance poet Langston Hughes described this lively part of Harlem's social and musical world, which took place

THE HARLEM RENAISSANCE

A new generation of writers who made Harlem their home—Langston Hughes, Zora Neale Hurston, Claude McKay, and James Weldon Johnson, among others—were both publishing their own journals and getting their work published by mainstream publishers. For the very first time, the work of African American writers and thinkers—poetry, fiction, essays, and books about race, politics, and social issues—was reaching a large audience.

The literary Harlem Renaissance overlapped with "Harlemania." The success of *Shuffle Along*, the first all-black Broadway musical featuring jazz music and jazz dances, sparked an interest in what was going on uptown. Thousands of New Yorkers came to Harlem to go clubbing and to hear the sounds of blues and jazz in Harlem's famous nightspots. The influence of the great black writers and entertainers working in Harlem in the 1920s stretched way beyond the 25 square blocks that made up Harlem proper.

Make Corn Bread for a Rent Party

SOME OF THE best music in Harlem took place at "parlor socials" or house rent parties. But the Harlem rent parties were also famous for "soul food," traditional home-cooked dishes from the Southern states. For an extra fee—as little as a quarter—guests could eat huge portions of fried chicken or fish, gumbo, chili, collard greens, and corn bread. Try out this recipe yourself for a simple, delicious quick bread that's great for snacking, dinner, or a party.

Adult supervision required

Makes 12 pieces

UTENSILS

- ♪ Measuring cups, measuring spoons,
- ♪ Large mixing bowl
- ♪ Medium mixing bowl
- ♪ 9 x 12-inch baking pan or 13-inch cast-iron frying pan

INGREDIENTS

- ♪ ¼ cup melted butter
- ♪ 1½ cups yellow cornmeal
- ♪ 2 cups unbleached flour
- ♪ 1 tablespoon baking powder
- ♪ 1 teaspoon baking soda
- ♪ 1 teaspoon salt
- ♪ 2 cups plain yogurt
- ♪ ½ cup milk
- ♪ ¼ cup brown sugar
- ♪ 2 eggs
- ♪ ½ cup fresh blueberries or fresh cooked corn kernels (optional)

1. Preheat the oven to 350 degrees.

2. Spread a little extra butter or cooking oil over a 9 x 13-inch baking pan, or (even better) a big cast-iron frying pan.

3. Mix together all the dry ingredients in a big mixing bowl. In another medium-size bowl, mix all the liquid ingredients, and beat in the eggs until smooth.

4. Pour the wet ingredients into the bowl of dry ingredients. Stir the batter until everything is blended together.

5. For an optional surprise, add ½ cup of blueberries or fresh cooked corn kernels.

6. Pour the batter into the baking pan or frying pan and bake for 25 to 30 minutes; when a toothpick poked into the center comes out clean, the corn bread is done.

7. Allow the corn bread to cool for 10 to 15 minutes. Cut into squares and serve while still warm.

"in small apartments where God knows who lived—because the guests seldom did—but where the piano would often be augmented by a guitar, or an odd cornet, or somebody with a pair of drums walking in off the street."

The admission price to a rent party was anywhere from 10 cents to a dollar. For this, you could hear great music, eat good food, and dance. You could also drink liquor, which was still illegal. But even for the rent party jobs, Duke was up against stiff competition. Harlem's finest stride pianists—James P. Johnson, Willie "The Lion" Smith, and the young Fats Waller—were in demand for these events and would receive the biggest tips.

Though they loved Harlem's excitement and glamour, after a few weeks Duke, Sony, and Otto grew tired of their hand-to-mouth adventure. One day Duke found some money on the street, and the three of them took the train back home to Washington, D.C.

Was the whole trip a mistake? No—it had fired up Duke's determination to be famous. Now he had seen New York City and its musicians first hand and had a better idea of just how good those musicians were. For the moment, Duke got right back into the life he'd led before his trip—playing gigs, getting gigs for other bands, being reunited with his wife and son, and even painting some signs. But he knew New York was the place to be.

Jazz pianist Fats Waller (left) and the legendary tap dancer Bill "Bojangles" Robinson (right). Institute of Jazz Studies

Within a few weeks—maybe sooner than Duke would have preferred—another opportunity in New York City came up. A vaudeville dancer named Clarence Robinson traveling through Washington heard Ellington with a band led by the banjo player Elmer Snowden. Robinson decided to use Snowden's group instead of the one he had been performing with. He promised them plenty of work if they came to New York City, and they agreed to join him. Snowden, Arthur Whetsel, Sonny Greer, and Otto Hardwick traveled ahead of Duke, who wanted their assurance that there was work for them. But when Duke arrived, the job with Robinson had evaporated—not an uncommon thing in vaudeville circles. This time there were five young musicians with no work and no money.

The Washingtonians: (left to right) Sonny Greer, Charlie Irvis, Otto "Toby" Hardwick, Elmer Snowden, Bubber Miley, Duke Ellington. Institute of Jazz Studies

Elmer Snowden took on the leadership of the group, and they started going around to auditions. After scuffling along for about a month, the band finally got a break. A singer named Ada Smith liked them and convinced her boss to hire them as her backup band at an elegant club in Harlem. This job finally put the band on the New York City musical map.

Barron Wilkins' Exclusive Club was a members-only club that catered to whites and light-skin blacks. The environment was very different from the rent parties and clubs that Duke had seen on his first trip. Barron Wilkins' club served expensive food and high-quality illegal liquor. Gangsters were regular customers and at times completely took over the place. This was not unusual. Gangsters were the major bootleggers, or smugglers of illegal liquor, and the worlds of entertainment and crime overlapped. For this job, the band played in a style that people used to call "sweet music." This was perfect for the club's atmosphere—sophisticated and on the quiet side, not the wilder style that was beginning to be known as "hot jazz." Duke worked long hours: the band started at 11:00 P.M. and played all through the night. But they were finally making steady money; each band member got $30 a week in salary and at least $20 a night in tips.

After a few weeks, Duke was settled enough to send for his wife Edna, but they decided to leave their son Mercer with Duke's parents for a while longer. They rented a room from Leonard Harper, a talented Harlem-based choreographer who gave Ellington another good job, as pianist for rehearsals for a new show. The show was for a new nightclub that was to open in the summer of 1923 called Connie's Inn. The club was designed to be the swankiest of all the Harlem places, and was to be open to both black and white customers, a "black and tan cabaret." As rehearsal pianist, Ellington was now part of the exciting process of bringing all the elements of a show together—the music, the dances, and creating a fantastic atmosphere. This experience was one of the keys to his future.

Finally, Ellington was feeling like a true working New York musician, and experienced Harlem in all its finery. He went to after-hours clubs, where musicians played all night, and heard a variety of the latest music. But he was also exploring other sides of the musical world in New York. New York City, unlike Washington, D.C., was home to the music business. New York was where all the music publishing companies and record companies were located. Record companies were churning out three-minute 78 rpms, and a new radio medium was expanding. So, in addition to performing, there were several avenues a talented and versatile musician could take to

pursue his dreams. Duke was interested in all of them.

Duke met a songwriter named Jo Trent, a lyricist, who introduced him to the world of Tin Pan Alley. Tin Pan Alley was the nickname of a street where hundreds of sheet music publishers had their offices. On 28th Street, off of Fifth Avenue, all day long songwriters and lyricists churned out songs in offices large and small. Duke and Jo's songs were

TIN PAN ALLEY

In the late 19th century, New York City was already a center for music publishing, songwriters, and composers. Many music publishers had their offices on the same block, West 28th Street between Broadway and Sixth Avenue in Manhattan. Early on, this block acquired the nickname "Tin Pan Alley," and some of the greatest American songwriters—Irving Berlin, Cole Porter, Jerome Kern, James P. Johnson, Fats Waller, and, later, Duke Ellington—sold their songs to publishers there; the composer George Gershwin got his start there, demonstrating other people's tunes. The most common story about how Tin Pan Alley got its name was the one written by a newspaper reporter in the early 1900s, who was asked to report on the sheet music business. He wrote that as he was heading down 28th Street toward all the music publishing offices, he heard the clanging sounds of many pianos playing different songs all at once through the open windows. To him, it sounded like a bunch of tin pans clanging. Tin Pan Alley remained a center for music publishing through the early 1950s.

often met with rejection but the pair still spent their days running around to Tin Pan Alley's jungle of offices, where a mishmash of songs and melodies could be heard being played on many pianos at the same time. Everyone hoped their song would be the one to catch a big publisher's ear.

Exciting as all of this was, Duke could see that the music business was extremely competitive and filled with ups and downs. For now, the band was under Elmer Snowden's leadership and consisted of Snowden, Duke Ellington, Sonny Greer, Otto Hardwick, and Arthur Whetsel. Snowden's Novelty Orchestra managed to get hired to make a couple of records for an important record label, RCA Victor, but the company decided not to release them. The partnerships even then—between song publishers, record companies, and radio executives—made up the strong force of the music business that still exists today, even with the Internet!

In September 1923, the band got another lucky break. They were hired to play at a club in midtown Manhattan called the Hollywood Club, on Broadway and 49th Street, right near all the Broadway theaters. Despite the glamorous name, the club was actually a dingy basement with a tiny bandstand under some exposed pipes. Duke sat at the piano right in front of the bandstand, where dancers jostled into him. But the club had a terrific location, right near Times Square, the heart of the entertainment district in New York City. As things turned out, this tiny bandstand would be the band's prime performance space for almost four years—and the launching pad for fame.

During the band's first few months at the Hollywood Club, there were several changes in the group's personnel. Even before they started their new job, the trumpet player Arthur Whetsel decided to return to Washington, D.C. to go to college. A new trumpet player was hired. James "Bubber" Miley completely changed the band's sound—from sweet jazz to hot. Just the same age as Duke, Miley had already played with some important blues and jazz bands, including Mamie Smith and Her Jazz Hounds. Miley played the trumpet in a very different style than Whetsel, whose sound was sweet and smooth. Bubber had learned how to use different mutes for his trumpet, which enabled him to get many different kinds of sounds from the horn: voice-like growls and wah-wah sounds. He was also a great improviser. Miley quickly became the star of the band, and other musicians often stopped by to hear him.

Soon, Snowden and Duke thought they should hire an additional horn player to keep up with the size of other bands. They found

Activity
String Theory—Build an Autoharp

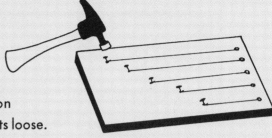

DURING THE JAZZ Age, jazz music was actually still in a pioneering stage. You might hear several instruments in a jazz dance band that you might not hear today, such as tuba, violin, rhythm guitar, and banjo. Musicians like Bubber Miley and composers like Duke Ellington liked to explore different sounds and combinations of sounds. Try your hand at making a simple autoharp to explore how sound is produced, and how to create different pitches (notes) on a stringed instrument.

YOU'LL NEED

- ♪ A smooth wooden board (the kind used for shelves), ³/₄ x 10 x 16 inches
- ♪ Ruler
- ♪ Pencil
- ♪ Clear nylon thread or fishing line, at least 2 yards
- ♪ Scissors
- ♪ Hammer
- ♪ 10 1-inch nails
- ♪ 1-inch wooden block
- ♪ Short metal or wooden ruler or bar

1. Take the piece of wood and, using the ruler, draw a straight line down the left side of the board along the 10-inch side.

2. Measure an inch down your straight line, and make 5 pencil marks, leaving about an inch between each mark.

3. Cut the nylon string into 5 pieces, measuring these lengths: 14 inches, 12 inches, 10 inches, 8 inches, and 6 inches.

4. Hammer five nails into your 5 pencil marks; drive the nails ½ inch into the board on your marks; try to hammer the nails in as straight as you can. One half of the nail will be left out.

5. Make a slipknot on both ends of the longest piece of nylon string, leaving the knots loose.

6. Put one knot over the top nail, and pull it as tightly as you can. Put a nail through the other slipknot, while you keep pulling really tightly. Hammer that nail into the wood along a straight line from the first nail, keeping the string as taut as you can.

7. Repeat steps 5 and 6 with the other four pieces of string.

Now your autoharp is ready to play. Pluck each string with your second finger. Does each string have a different pitch (note)? Which string makes the highest sound? Which one makes the lowest? You will find that the longer the string, the lower the pitch; the shorter the string, the higher the pitch.

Now take the 1-inch block and place it under the middle of the longest string. Pluck the string on both sides of the block. What kind of notes do you get? Experiment by moving the blocks to different parts of all the strings. You can also play this instrument by strumming the strings together. See what kinds of sounds you get when you hold a ruler or metal bar along all the strings and strum.

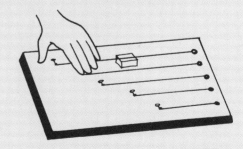

Banjo player and guitarist Fred Guy (left) with Duke, 1925. Institute of Jazz Studies

trombonist Charlie Irvis, who really liked the different sounds that Miley got with mutes; he soon started using them himself on trombone. The band's sound changed dramatically. "Our band changed character when Bubber came in," Ellington said. "He used to growl all night long, playing gutbucket on his horn. That was when we decided to forget all about the sweet music."

In the midst of all these changes, the band got its first review. In the fall of 1923, Abel Green wrote about the band in *The Clipper*, an entertainment paper, and singled out Bubber Miley:

"This colored band is plenty torrid and includes a trumpet player who never need doff his chapeau to any cornetist in the business. He exacts the eeriest sort of modulations and 'singing' notes heard. . . .The boys look neat in dress suits and labor hard but not in vain at their music. They disclose painstaking rehearsal, playing without music . . ."

The writer also describes how they each played a couple of different instruments. Bubber played trumpet and mellophone, Snowden played banjo and soprano sax, the trombonist also played trumpet, and drummer Sonny Greer also sang.

But in early 1924, Snowden left the group. At first Duke thought it was because Snowden didn't really like the band's new style—hot and growly, instead of sweet. But Snowden was having arguments with Sonny Greer, who accused him of taking too much extra pay for himself as the group's leader. Soon the other members found out and were angry, too. Sonny and the other musicians thought that Duke would be the best person for the new leader. After all, Duke had been their bandleader in Washington and was very good at doing business—which meant getting more work, making sure the band got paid, and being fair to all.

Under Duke's leadership the band started attracting more attention. Snowden was replaced by Fred Guy, who played banjo and guitar, which added a new sound to the band. One thing that really helped the band get exposure was radio. Like many other nightclubs and dance halls in the mid-1920s, the Hollywood Club installed a radio wire. People could hear broadcasts from the club in many cities around the country. And, as a listener at home, how would you know that the Hollywood Club was a tiny club in a basement instead of a big fancy nightclub? Starting in early 1924, every night (very late) and on Wednesday afternoon, you could hear the music of Duke and his friends on the radio under a new name: Duke Ellington and His Washingtonians. ∞

4

THE WASHINGTONIANS HIT THE BIG TIME

*I*t is easy to forget how much was brand-new in the 1920s, a decade in which new technology became part of almost every aspect of life. Automobiles were now common, most households had telephones, and tabletop radios and the phonograph were replacing pianos as families' home-entertainment systems. America had become a modern country with a youth culture that wanted to go out and dance.

Jazz was the music that was meant for dancing—whether the dance was the flashy Charleston, the acrobatic Lindy Hop (named after Charles Lindbergh's historic transatlantic solo airplane flight in 1927), or the romantic fox trot. Fortunately for Duke and other bandleaders, the dance craze, born just 10 years earlier, showed no signs of being a passing fad. If anything, dancing was more popular than ever. Ballrooms and dance halls kept springing up all over the country, in big cities and small towns. This meant steady jobs for dance bands, whether they had a famous bandleader or were just an OK band that played the latest songs.

The very best bands could earn money in several ways. They could go on the road to perform at stage shows in big movie palaces and theaters, and along their tour play at local ballrooms and dance halls. If a band really caught on, it could become the "house band" and stay at a place for weeks, or even years. Some of these jobs gave the bands a lot of exposure in the nightclubs and ballrooms that had radio wires. Radio broadcasting and record sales boomed during the 1920s, spreading music more quickly than ever before. All these trends and innovations helped Duke and his band.

But the Jazz Age had a dark side, too. Nightclubs like the Hollywood Club, where Duke and his band worked, were typically owned by gangsters, the same gangsters who controlled the big-money business of selling illegal alcohol to their patrons. Sometimes, a powerful mobster liked a particular band and wanted them to play all night—or else. This turned some musical situations into "command performances." Musicians were also often counted on to act as a cover for illegal drinking. One of Sonny Greer's jobs at the Hollywood Club,

Sheet music cover for "Black and Tan Fantasy." Courtesy Morris Hodara in addition to being Ellington's drummer, was to tip off the Hollywood staff when anyone suspicious came in asking for liquor.

Meanwhile, Duke Ellington and His Washingtonians were becoming better known in midtown Manhattan. They started performing an early show at the nearby Cinderella Ballroom that attracted customers to come hear them at the Hollywood. They went on their very first tour on the dance band circuit, up to Massachusetts and New England. Back in New York City that fall, Duke and a couple of his musicians hit another milestone and recorded seven single 78 rpms. On five of them they accompanied singers; but two of them were under the Washingtonians' own name, playing Duke's original tunes. These first two records of Duke's own compositions were "Choo-Choo," the first of many train tunes that Duke would write, and "Rainy Nights."

Duke knew that composing and recording new material with his band would set it apart from so many others. He also knew that composing songs that were published and then performed by others would give his musical career an added special dimension, and possibly earn him extra money as well. During the day he continued to work with Jo Trent, a more experienced songwriter, brainstorming lyrics and melodies to try to sell to the music publishers in Tin Pan Alley.

Courtesy David Hajdu

Duke was also learning how to arrange music for his band. Now that his band had three horns, they needed more specific musical arrangements. Musical arrangements are a way to assign parts to the different instruments to harmonize the leading melody part, or come up with accompaniments for the other horns to play. All of this was new and exciting, and Duke continued to keep his ears wide open to learn from what the other bandleaders and arrangers around him were doing. Customized arrangements were also a way to make a band sound unique, in contrast to the many bands that used "stock arrangements" or "stocks," which were simplified arrangements for bands sold by music publishers.

Duke discovered how to create color and drama by combining instruments in an unusual way. For instance, he would have a low instrument like the trombone play the melody, with higher harmony parts for clarinet and trumpet soaring over the melody. He also had two or three instruments play notes close together that sometimes sounded wrong, but had a great effect.

By 1925, with Bubber Miley as a star attraction and playing original compositions and arrangements, Duke Ellington and His Washingtonians were getting a reputation as a band with a unique sound. Still, just as Duke had done during his early days as a bandleader in Washington, D.C., he continued to befriend more experienced musicians. One of them was Will Marion Cook, a respected African American composer and conductor who was 30 years older than Duke. Cook was a conservatory-educated musician who moved easily between the concert hall, musical theater, and Tin Pan Alley. He gave Duke a lot of advice, and even recommended that Duke get some conservatory training. When Duke resisted that advice, Cook then told him: "First you find the logical way, and when you find it, avoid it, and let your inner self break through and guide you. Don't try to be anybody else

Whitey's Lindy Hoppers, one of the most sensational professional groups of Lindy Hoppers; most of the dancers were first seen at the Savoy Ballroom in Harlem. Institute of Jazz Studies

Dance the Lindy Hop

WHAT MADE THE big band era so fabulous? The music was meant for dancing, and dancers and bands inspired each other to crazier rhythms and crazier steps. Trendy dances like the Charleston and the Turkey Trot kept people on their feet. But the Lindy Hop, which people started doing in 1927, was the most popular dance of all. People danced the Lindy Hop all the way through World War II. Teenagers used the basic Lindy step when they started dancing to rock 'n' roll in the 1950s. And though many Lindy Hoppers were acrobatic and made up really wild routines, the basic Lindy step is simple and easy to learn. Try this with a friend.

YOU'LL NEED

♪ A partner

♪ Dance music (see suggestions)

♪ CD player, computer, iPod, or other music listening device

Listen to one of the suggested recordings. Then try the basic step, which you do to 6 counts: step (1, 2), step (3, 4), back, step (5, 6). You will be stepping in place, shifting your weight with each step. See if you can keep this up through most of the tune. Now try it with your partner. Face your partner (girl on right side, boy on left); you can either hold both of your partner's hands, or place the girl's right hand in the boy's left, with your other arm circling your partner. The boy's first step will always be with his left foot, and the girl's will be her right foot.

Counts 1 and 2: The boy steps out with his left foot, the girl with her right.

Counts 3 and 4: Boy shifts to right foot, while girl shifts to left.

Counts 5 and 6: Boy steps back on left foot, then steps on right; girl steps back on right foot, then steps on left.

Once you and your partner get the hang of this, you can twirl or improvise!

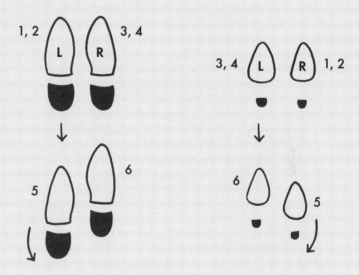

Favorite Lindy Hop Records

Here are some of the top swing dance tunes that have the perfect beat for the Lindy Hop.

Duke Ellington: "It Don't Mean a Thing (If It Ain't Got That Swing)"; "Rockin' in Rhythm"; "Take the 'A' Train"

Benny Goodman: "Christopher Columbus"; "Stompin' at the Savoy"

Count Basie: "One O'Clock Jump"; "Lady Be Good"; "April in Paris"

Erskine Hawkins: "Tuxedo Junction"

but yourself." Within a few short years, this is what Duke Ellington was able to do. His music had an individualized sound and feeling that would only grow stronger.

The rough-and-tumble world of music in New York City was full of surprises. In early 1925, there was a fire in the Hollywood Club, and it was shut down for a couple of months to be repaired. This might not have been an accident. Sometimes club owners, some of whom were gangsters, arranged for accidents or fires to happen so they could collect the insurance money. The club reopened in March with a new name—the Kentucky Club, and the Washingtonians reclaimed their place on the small stage.

The band worked hard every night. They played music for dancing from 9:00 P.M. until midnight, and also backed up floor shows, revues, and singers. In addition to their original tunes, the Washingtonians also played popular dance tunes of the day, such as "Whispering," "Avalon," and "St. Louis Blues." But even for these familiar songs, Duke did not want the band to play stock arrangements. At Duke's insistence (also because his musicians were not all such great sight-readers), the band made up their own arrangements. Sonny Greer used to say that Duke would "take the popular tunes and twist them." Their arrangements had a give-and-take quality that the other bands didn't have. "You write for their abilities and natural tendencies and give them places where they do their best—certain entrances and exits and background stuff," Duke explained. The musicians might come up with a riff as part of a background line. These early arrangements were probably more talked out than they were written out. Duke's collaborative method of arranging would be the basis of the Ellington band's sound for decades to come.

Duke and his men had stiff competition. The biggest stars of the dance band world at that time were Fletcher Henderson and the white bandleader Paul Whiteman. Whiteman and Henderson played at the best ballrooms, recorded frequently, and were broadcast wherever they went. Their arrangements, with call-and-response exchanges between the trumpets and the saxophones, for instance, became the standard model of the time. Good musical arrangements helped these bands sound clear above a crowd of dancers in the days before microphones.

Both Whiteman and Henderson hired the biggest jazz stars of the day. In the mid-1920s, Henderson's band featured the trumpet player Louis Armstrong, already a star, and Coleman Hawkins, whose big sound on the tenor saxophone made that instrument as popular as the trumpet. Whiteman's band included important soloists like the cornetist Bix Beiderbecke, trombonist Tommy Dorsey, and the great jazz violinist Joe Venuti. Whiteman also made jazz more "respectable" with his orchestra's 1924 premiere of George Gershwin's *Rhapsody in Blue,* bringing jazz into the concert hall for the first time.

Even so, Duke's band was making a name for itself. The Kentucky Club was the place where musicians and celebrities came to relax. Paul Whiteman himself came by to hear Duke's band, as did members of Fletcher Henderson's band. Sydney Bechet, a legendary New Orleans musician on soprano saxophone and clarinet, sat in with Duke's band one night; he liked their music so much that he ended up playing with them for several months. The band had a great spirit and soulful sound. Drummer Sonny Greer said:

The flavor was a once-in-a-lifetime thing. We worked as one man. Duke has the brains, always prodding us to do better, showing kindness and understanding. He was always with his men. While working on new things, he might be a bit distant. But then, after jotting his thoughts down on paper, Ellington would come out with us after the job a few nights running. He'd listen to the guys and get an idea of what they were thinking.

Activity
Experiment with Sound Effects

"BLACK AND TAN Fantasy" and "Creole Love Call" are two recordings by Ellington's band from 1927 that show how Bubber Miley and Tricky Sam sounded like talking horns. You can really hear their range of "wah-wah"s and growly sounds. To achieve these effects they used mutes—different shaped objects that fit over the bells of their horns, or into them. The plunger mute is the same shape as (you guessed it) a toilet plunger. A quick open-close motion of the mute over the bell of the horn is what produces the "wah-wah" sound. Straight mutes have a hollow, cone-shaped design that produces a metallic buzzing sound. You can make two simple wind instruments with materials from around the house, a jug and a kazoo, and explore similar talking-horn type sounds. Try making these with a friend.

MAKE A PLASTIC JUG TUBA

YOU'LL NEED
♪ A friend or two   ♪ Water
♪ 4 empty 12-ounce soda bottles, or ½-gallon milk containers

Rinse out the empty bottles to make sure they are clean. Hold the bottle up to your mouth, and press your lower lip below the very top of the bottle. Blow across the top of the bottle. Try this a few times until you can make a nice deep whistling sound. Then try putting about an inch of water in the bottle. Blow again. Is the sound lower or higher? Have your friend take a different bottle and try the same thing. Then, each of you takes two bottles and puts different amounts of water in three of them; leave one empty to produce the lowest sound.

Experiment with Sound Effects, *continued*

Experiment with the range of sounds you can get from four bottles, and make up a melody using those four notes. If you like, gather even more bottles and more friends, and with your new kazoo have a real jug band!

MAKE A KAZOO

YOU'LL NEED

- ♪ Hole punch
- ♪ Empty toilet paper or paper towel roll
- ♪ Scissors
- ♪ Waxed paper
- ♪ Rubber band
- ♪ Crayons or colored markers, or construction paper and glue

1. Using the hole punch, punch a hole in the empty roll, as far down from the end as the hole punch will reach.

2. Cut a circle out of waxed paper that is about an inch bigger around than the circumference of the roll. Wrap the waxed paper over one end of the roll, and fasten it around the end with a rubber band so that the wax paper is pretty tight and smooth.

3. Decorate with crayons, markers, or glue on colored pieces of paper in a pattern.

4. To play your kazoo, hum into the open end of the roll, allowing a little air to blow out through your mouth. The moving air will allow the waxed paper to vibrate, and the kazoo will produce a humming sound.

After hours at the Kentucky Club, when the other musicians had gone home, Duke and Sonny Greer would play as a duo, and raked in extra money in tips. This was the era of big-spending gangsters and businessmen. "Money was flying," said Greer about these days. "You better believe it. We had all the gangsters, all the big gangsters you read about, Legs Diamond, Lucky Luciano, and all the Brooklyn gang. They'd rendezvous."

"[The Kentucky Club] was a good place for us to be, because it stayed open all night and became a rendezvous for all the big stars and musicians on Broadway after they got through working."

This was the environment in which Duke became a showman and an entertainer—a crowd-pleaser who played what the audience wanted to hear, and always appeared elegant and cool.

In the fall of 1925, the band received a couple of really good reviews. A writer from *Billboard* magazine, one of the first music business magazines, wrote: "And now for the band! If anybody can tell us where a hotter aggregation than Duke Ellington and His Club Kentucky Serenaders [as the band was sometimes called] can be found, we'll buy for the mob."

Sometimes opportunities popped up, and Duke had to produce new music quickly. One day, his songwriting partner Jo Trent was in a hurry to find him. "Tonight, we've got to write a show," Trent said. "Tonight!" They immediately sat down and wrote four songs that were included in one of the all-black revues that were so popular at the time. The show was called *Chocolate Kiddies*.

Chocolate Kiddies never ran on Broadway, but its troupe took it to Europe, and it was a hit in Berlin, Copenhagen, Stockholm, and several other cities. Duke's songs were getting around. In post–World War I Europe, there was a demand for American jazz, popular dance, and everything related to black entertainment, especially after a dancer named Josephine Baker became the toast of Paris with her sensational *Revue Negre*. Even so, a 10-day ocean voyage to Europe was an awesome undertaking for the many entertainers who made the trip.

Meanwhile, at the Kentucky Club, Duke Ellington and His Washingtonians expanded as a group. A new trombone player came along who was the perfect match for Bubber Miley. Joe "Tricky Sam" Nanton had his own set of growls and mute effects. Miley and Nanton's range of sounds—their growls, wah-wahs, and laughing horns—attracted musicians from more famous bands to the Kentucky Club. Everything they did added to the music. "They were always blowing for each other and getting ideas for what they wanted to play," Duke once said.

THE WASHINGTONIANS ON TOUR

 During the summer of 1926, the band traveled to New England for its second tour as a dance band. They played in Boston and many small towns in Massachusetts and New Hampshire. Their first tour the year before had been a big success, and Charles Schribman, the tour organizer, was a big admirer of Duke's music. Advertisements called Duke's band "The Paul Whiteman of Colored Orchestras . . . known all over America as the hottest Band on Broadway."

Though it was great for the band to be out of sweltering New York City, this was no vacation. Duke's band traveled to a new town almost every day and competed in "band

"It was at the Kentucky Club that our music acquired new colors and characteristics."

(Clockwise from top) Fred Guy, Billy Taylor, Sonny Greer, and Wellman Braud. For a short while in the 1930s, Ellington had two bass players. Institute of Jazz Studies

battles" almost every night. Additionally, the Washingtonians followed in the footsteps of more famous bands on the same touring circuit. Duke wanted the band to sound their very best at every performance.

When Duke and the band returned to New York in the fall, they signed an eight-month contract at the Kentucky Club, the longest contract they had been offered. Two new musicians joined the band over the summer. One of the new members was saxophonist Harry Carney. Carney was from Boston and only 17 years old, but within a few years, he became legendary on his main instrument, the baritone saxophone. Duke also hired the band's first string bass player, Wellman Braud.

Around the same time, Irving Mills, an ambitious young businessman, entered Duke's life. Mills's family owned a music publishing company, and Irving was a clever manager and publicity agent. He immediately saw star potential in Duke Ellington and his band. From the very beginning of their business relationship, Mills's strategy was to present Ellington as a "great musician who was making a lasting contribution to American music."

Mills started to work wonders for the band, especially in getting their music more well-known. He got Duke and the band recording contracts with the two leading record companies of the time, Brunswick and Victor.

Additionally, Mills encouraged Ellington to compose more original material, which Duke and the band could then record.

After Duke made his first few records, he was hooked; he liked the process of making records and hearing what the band's music sounded like. He also realized the great exposure a hit record could bring him. He started spending at least a couple of hours a day working on new compositions and songs. This became a regular part of his day. As a creative person, composing and writing songs was both satisfying and challenging to Duke. Eventually, some of his compositions proved to be financially successful, too.

The months flew by. After a third summer tour of New England in 1927, the band returned to New York City. For the first time, Duke and the band did not return to the Kentucky Club. With Irving Mills's encouragement, Duke was ready for a change. Duke and the band got hired to play in three shows, one right after the other. The first was called *Jazzmania*, a stylish black revue with a fast-paced sequence of music, songs, dances, and comedy routines that proved to be a hit with black and white audiences. The cast included a beautiful singer named Adelaide Hall, and Ellington's band was a showstopper, too. One paper raved: "Both in the orchestra pit and on the stage their performance was superb. With

JAZZ ON RECORD

In the early 1900s, the very first recordings for gramophones were a great success. These included arias by the Italian tenor singer Enrico Caruso, "Stars and Stripes Forever" by John Philip Sousa's band, and novelty recordings such as the poem "Casey at the Bat." The very first jazz records, the "Livery Stable Blues" and "Tiger Rag" by the Original Dixieland Jazz Band in 1917, and "Japanese Sandman" and "Whisperin'" by Paul Whiteman's Orchestra in 1918, sold over a million copies each, setting off a popular music craze that boosted the brand-new recording industry through the 1920s.

Were the barnyard-inspired sounds of the Original Dixieland Jazz Band really jazz? Or would we think of Paul Whiteman's orchestrated dance music as jazz? Jazz music in the 1920s tumbled out of an assortment of regions with different sounds, influences, and developments. Almost any music with a strong rhythmic element was now called jazz, whether it was Louis Armstrong's fabulous improvisations or tinny dance music for the Charleston. Record companies such as RCA Victor, Okeh, and Columbia sought out talent as fiercely as miners sought gold during the gold rush.

The record companies realized there was a market for what they called "race records" and targeted recordings by blues and jazz artists to sell to stores in African American neighborhoods. Mamie Smith's recording of "Crazy Blues" in 1920 sold over a million copies in less than a year. She and Bessie Smith (no relation) often used jazz musicians in their backup groups. In those days, recording techniques were still primitive. The musicians played into a huge megaphone coming from a control room, the piano usually had a megaphone of its own, and drums were muffled with a blanket so that they wouldn't drown out everyone else. Needless, to say, the music did not always sound so great!

Duke Ellington and His Orchestra in the early 1930s.
Institute of Jazz Studies

the possible exception of Fletcher Henderson's band, Duke Ellington seems to head the greatest existing aggregation of colored musicians." *Jazzmania* was such a success that the show's organizers quickly put together a sequel called *Dancemania,* which was immediately booked for a tour. The first stop was to be a big theater in Philadelphia.

Right before Duke and the band left for the tour, they found themselves again "in the right place at the right time" to get their biggest break of all—a job at Harlem's most famous nightclub, the Cotton Club.

The Cotton Club had not had a steady house band for months after the previous bandleader died suddenly. Two or three other leaders had been offered the job but did not take it. The club's managers were worried about maintaining the Cotton Club's reputation as Harlem's most elite nightspot. They wanted to ensure they could open a new show in December 1927.

Jimmy McHugh, a songwriter for several shows at the Cotton Club, liked Duke's band and knew that *Dancemania* was due to go on the road. He took the Cotton Club's managers to hear Duke's band the night before they were to go to Philadelphia. The manager was so impressed that he asked Duke and his band to be the band for the next Cotton Club revue. Duke signed a contract on the spot.

The following day, Duke and his band and the *Dancemania* troupe took off. During their second week in Philadelphia, a local gangster named "Boo Boo" Hoff, who was connected to the mobsters who owned the Cotton Club, showed up at the theater. He came by to get Duke released from his Philadelphia contract so that Duke and the band could start rehearsals back in New York. Hoff's words to the manager of the Philadelphia Theater were: "Be big or you'll be dead." In this sense, "be big" meant be generous—let Duke out of his contract. Hoff, a huge "don't-mess-with-me" type, was big enough himself to let Duke and his musicians finish out the week. Once again, Harlem beckoned. ∞

5

FROM THE COTTON CLUB TO THE WORLD

Duke Ellington and His Orchestra made their debut at the Cotton Club on December 4, 1927. The dancers in their feathered costumes got far more attention than Duke's band did on that first night, but Duke's nights at the Cotton Club soon set him on his way to stardom.

The Cotton Club, Harlem's most famous nightspot, was the prime destination for New Yorkers and tourists in-the-know who wanted to go somewhere sophisticated, modern, and in step with the Jazz Age. As one British musician said: "It was expensive and it was exclusive; it cost you the earth merely to look at the girl who took your hat and coat as you went in. It was run by a white man for white patrons who sincerely believed that when they visited the place they were seeing Harlem at its most authentic."

From its opening in September 1923 until it relocated to midtown in 1939, the Cotton Club was a showcase for the world's greatest African American entertainers: dancers such as Earl "Snake Hips" Tucker and the Nicholas Brothers, singers such as Adelaide Hall and Ethel Waters, and three of the best big bands of all time: Duke Ellington's (1927–1931), Cab Calloway's (1930–1933), and Jimmie Lunceford's (1934–1936).

The Cotton Club shows were sensational, for audience and performers alike. The chief ingredients for their success were the nonstop pace, great timing, and all the beautiful dancers and elaborate sets. Everything—a top-billed singer or comedian, a fabulously dressed chorus line, comedy sketches, specialty acts, and Duke's band with their talking, growling horns—was packed into a 90-minute show, performed two or three times a night. Everyone involved had to be the best at their game.

There were two new revues produced every year for the 16 years that the club was located in Harlem, and some of these shows went on to become Broadway productions. Dan Healy was the club's main choreographer and director. Duke not only performed and led the band, he wrote new dance music as well as music for introductions, transitions, and accompaniments.

But the Cotton Club was a fantasyland filled with contradictions. The club, which could seat about 700 people, had a whites-only admissions policy (though it admitted black celebrities), making it off-limits to most Harlem residents. Meanwhile the entire staff and all the entertainers were black. The stage set was a replica of a Southern mansion, and Duke and his musicians performed on the veranda in front of a painted backdrop of willow trees and slave cabins. Today we would view this as stereotypical and even racist, but for Duke, his musicians, and all the chorus girls and entertainers who worked there, a job at the Cotton Club was considered prestigious and a great opportunity.

Cab Calloway, another famous bandleader whose band took over when Duke and his band left the Cotton Club in February 1931,

Activity
Make Costumes for a Floor Show

THE SHOWS AT the Cotton Club and other nightclubs were called "floor shows" because the dancers and singers performed on the floor in front of the stage, which was reserved for the band. The tables were arranged in a horseshoe shape to allow plenty of room for the performers. The shows had themes, with costumes and accessories that went along with them. There were shows with "Wild West" themes and plenty of "jungle" themed shows, with leopard-skin costumes. Some of the costumes were not so wild: tap dancers like the Nicholas Brothers appeared in tuxedos, and a crisp-looking top hat was a great accessory. The Cotton Club dancers often wore feathered costumes, complete with feathered arm and ankle bracelets. Try making these accessories yourself.

MAKE A TOP HAT

Adult supervision required

YOU'LL NEED

- ♪ 2 large sheets of stiff black construction paper
- ♪ Ruler
- ♪ Pencil
- ♪ Scissors
- ♪ Exacto knife
- ♪ Stapler
- ♪ Scotch tape

1. Using one of the large sheets of paper, measure out a rectangle, approximately 8 x 20 inches.

2. Shape it into an 8-inch-high cylinder that will fit snugly around your head;

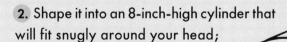

the hole will be more of an oblong than a circle. Staple or tape the edge to keep the cylinder shape.

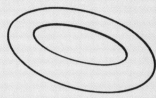

3. Trace around the cylinder on the other sheet of paper, then draw another oblong parallel to the first, to make a hat brim that is 3 inches wide. Keep the oblong cutout.

4. Attach the cylinder to the brim with tape; then attach the oblong shape to the top using tape.

5. If you like, make a decorative hat band.

MAKE FEATHERED ARM AND ANKLE BRACELETS

YOU'LL NEED

- ♪ Small roll of 1-inch-wide, adhesive-backed Velcro
- ♪ Scissors
- ♪ Bag of colored feathers
- ♪ Various small decorations such as sequins, buttons, and glitter

1. Leaving the adhesive backing in place and keeping the two layers together, cut 2 Velcro strips to a length that allows you to wrap them comfortably around your wrists, adding approximately 1 extra inch to form fasteners. In the same way, cut 2 strips to go around your ankles.

continued...

61

Activity

Make Costumes for a Floor Show, continued

2. Take one of the strips and pull the two layers apart. Lay the "hooks" layer down on a table with the hooks facing up. Line that layer with a row of feathers, attaching the quill end of the feathers to the Velcro. Leave 1 inch on one end of the strip free of feathers.

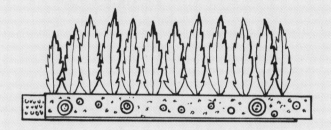

3. Press the "loops" layer of the Velcro down over the feathers, overlapping the feathered piece so that 1 inch of Velcro is exposed at each end. The feathers should now be firmly sandwiched between the two pieces of Velcro.

4. Peel the adhesive backing off one of the layers, and firmly press your decorations on to the adhesive.

5. Repeat the steps above with the three remaining Velcro strips, creating two bracelets and two anklets altogether. Wrap them around your wrists and ankles, pressing the exposed ends of Velcro together to fasten.

often spoke about what it meant to be an entertainer there:

> It's no accident that the name Cotton Club has come to be synonymous with the greatest Negro entertainment of the twenties and thirties. . . . A lot of people worked hard to put those shows together. . . . That was the Cotton Club spirit. Work, work, work. Rehearse, rehearse, and rehearse. Get it down fine. Tops and professional in every sense of the word. . . . If the chorus line wasn't rehearsing, then the band was. If the band wasn't rehearsing, then the act was . . . We knew we couldn't miss a lick. And we rarely did.

The Cotton Club was a great place for Duke Ellington and his band, even though the band got off to a slightly rocky start. To keep the job the band had to expand to 11 members, and the new musicians had to learn to blend in right away. All in all, Duke and His Cotton Club Orchestra (as the band was now sometimes known) fit right into the club's exotic atmosphere. Jazz historian Marshall Stearns described a show at the club:

> The floor shows at the Cotton Club . . . were an incredible mishmash of talent and nonsense. I recall one where a light-skinned and

magnificently muscled Negro burst through a papier-mâché jungle onto the dance floor, clad in an aviator's helmet, goggles and shorts. He proceeded to rescue a blonde being worshipped by the natives. . . . In the background, Bubber Miley, Tricky Sam and other members of the Ellington band growled, wheezed and snorted.

Duke Ellington, who had never set foot on a plantation or in a jungle, was soon the master of "jungle music." What was jungle music as imagined by Duke? Some of Duke's arrangements for the Club used a heavy tom-tom beat by Sonny Greer, and Bubber Miley pulled out his most dramatic wah-wahs and growls.

Every few months there was a new show with a wild and exotic theme—the jungle, the Deep South, the Wild West. Duke composed and arranged background music for these shows, whose songs were written by the great team of Jimmy McHugh and Dorothy Fields. Duke also composed music for the specialty acts, novelty dancers, the chorus line, and his own featured spots. The pace was crazy. The club opened at 10:00 P.M., just in time to entertain an after-theater crowd; "All Broadway comes to Harlem" pronounced one advertisement. Ellington's band played for dancing before and after the floor shows (the second show usually started at midnight). The

club stayed open until 3:00 A.M., and some of Duke's musicians then went to other Harlem nightspots for after-hours jam sessions.

Duke thrived on these challenges and meanwhile became a master showman himself, conducting his band from the piano. He learned to take the pulse of his audience. Every night he could see which of his new tunes caught on, which didn't, and what people liked to dance to.

It didn't take too long for Duke's band to have the unified, swinging sound that would define it for decades. More than ever, Duke

Cab Calloway, another great Cotton Club bandleader. Institute of Jazz Studies

63

The saxophonist Harry Carney was born in Boston in 1910. In late summer of 1927 Carney subbed in Duke's band. Duke wanted to hire him but had to convince Carney's parents to let their son join his band, and promised to act as the 17-year-old's guardian. Carney played all saxophones but eventually settled on the biggest of all, the baritone saxophone. He once said, "I wanted to impress everyone with the idea that the baritone was necessary." Carney joined the band a few months before its debut at the Cotton Club. His mastery of the baritone saxophone was very influential to other jazz big bands. Thanks to him, the baritone sax became the anchor of the saxophone section in the leading big bands of the 1930s and 1940s. Carney died in 1974, a few months after Duke did. He had played with Duke's band for over 45 years.

Drummer Sonny Greer was born in New Jersey in 1895. He worked with Duke Ellington from 1920 until the early 1950s, and was a great asset to the band for his genial showmanship as well as his play-ing. When Greer moved with the band to the Cotton Club, a drum company supplied him with what looked like a pyramid of drums and other percussion instruments—gongs, chimes, and even timpani. Greer died in 1982, and like Harry Carney was one of the rare long-term bandmates that outlived Duke.

Johnny Hodges, Duke's star on alto saxophone.
Institute of Jazz Studies

Alto saxophonist Johnny Hodges, born in 1907, was a childhood friend of Harry Carney's from Boston. When Duke hired him in 1928, Hodges had already developed a beautiful sound. His nickname in Duke's band was "Rabbit," because he really liked lettuce sandwiches. Hodges's gorgeous sound on alto saxophone was the heart of the band, and except for a couple of years in the 1950s, he played with Duke until his death in 1970.

Trumpet player Cootie Williams, born in Alabama in 1910, was already an in-demand New York mu-

tailored his material to the strengths and personalities of his musicians. He was still acquiring the skills as an arranger to write out the musicians' parts quickly. This would come in time, but during rehearsals he would sing the individual parts to his musicians. They learned almost everything on the spot by ear, and there was a lot of give-and-take between Duke and his musicians.

Between 1927 and 1929, there were several personnel changes in the band, which brought it up to 12 members. The band had a fantastic collective and collaborative spirit. Duke and his men were in this together—and were well on their way to becoming famous together, too.

For Duke's younger musicians, like 17-year-old Harry Carney, the baritone saxophone player, the weekly pay of $75 was a fortune, and some of that went back to his family in Boston. Duke tried to convince alto saxophonist Johnny Hodges, a childhood friend of Harry's from Boston, to join the band in May 1928 after Toby Hardwick was in a bad taxicab accident and couldn't play for a while. Johnny was already part of the dance band scene in New York and had been working at the Savoy Ballroom, the "Home of Happy Feet," and other Harlem hotspots. Hodges's warm sound on alto sax became a signature sound of the band, especially on slow romantic songs. Altogether, the woodwind section with Hodges, Carney, and clarinetist Barney Bigard was shaping up as one of the most unusual of any dance band.

Duke's manager, Irving Mills, capitalized on Duke's job at the Cotton Club right away. Mills wanted to help Duke earn more money and also get more exposure. Technology was one way to do this. A friend of Mills convinced someone at CBS, then a new national radio network, to broadcast live from the Cotton

Dancing Rope Trick

DURING THE JAZZ Age, nightclubs like the Cotton Club typically had tableside entertainers in addition to the lavish floor shows, chorus dancers, and music. Magicians, fortune tellers, and card players wandered around the club performing feats of magic and card tricks, and telling fortunes at the tables of the wealthy patrons. This is a mini-version of a famous ancient dancing rope trick. Try this at your dinner table, and amaze your friends and family.

YOU'LL NEED
- ♪ Pocket comb
- ♪ Ball of wool yarn
- ♪ 12-inch piece of cotton thread

Rub the comb briskly with the wool to give the comb a strong electro-static charge. Put the wool aside. Now take the cotton thread in your right hand so that about 6 inches of thread is left hanging loose. Bring the comb to the free end of the thread so that it just touches the comb. Then draw the comb up vertically very slowly, so that the comb becomes separated from the thread. Eureka! You can make the thread stand up by itself, even when it is about 1/2 inch away from the comb. Move the comb around in a small figure eight; the thread should follow the motion of the comb (this might take some practice). This is the ancient dancing rope trick, in miniature!

Club. These national broadcasts made Duke Ellington and His Cotton Club Orchestra an overnight sensation. People all across the country tuned in to hear Duke's band, as well as the emcee's gossip about the famous people who came to dance, dine, and be seen. Duke and the band also broadcast at dinnertime during a weekly dinner-hour dance, which became a radio favorite during the late 1920s. Sonny Greer said: "Everybody was waiting for that, from New York to California.... Of course, you know that's suppertime. All the people, nobody got anything to eat until we got off. Cats working all day starved to death until we got off."

Meanwhile, Irving Mills kept encouraging Duke to write more compositions and record them with the band. Mills then published the sheet music, often with his own name as co-composer. Mills was Duke's manager, and also his booking agent, music publisher, record producer, and ceaseless promoter; for all of these activities, Mills paid himself a generous percentage of whatever Duke's fee was. Irving Mills made a lot of money from the talents and hard work of his ever-more-famous client, and became a powerful figure in the entertainment business.

Duke churned out new tunes and arrangements, urged on by the constant need for new material at the club and for record dates—jungle music for the shows, fast dance numbers or moody ballads for dancing. His band members helped him do this, especially Bubber Miley. Miley was not only the band's most important soloist, he was also a good composer. Between 1927 and 1929, Miley and Duke co-composed some of the band's most important pieces to date: "East St. Louis Toodle-O," "Creole Love Call," and "Black and Tan Fantasy." "East St. Louis Toodle-O" was an up-tempo dance number that became the band's theme song for the next 12 years. Duke and Bubber Miley had imaginary stories behind their music. Duke described one tune like this: "This is an old man, tired of working in the field since sunup, coming up the road in the sunset on his way home to dinner; he's tired but strong. . . ."

Even though Miley contributed so much to the band, in 1929 Duke told Miley to leave. Miley had become more and more dependent on alcohol and was unreliable. He missed recording dates, showed up late for performances, and was often drunk. This was a huge loss; after all it was Bubber's style that had helped turn the Washingtonians into a band that was good enough to play at the Cotton Club. Duke did not fire people lightly—in fact, throughout his whole career, there were only one or two people that he actually fired.

Duke hired 18-year-old Cootie Williams, then playing with Fletcher Henderson's band, to take Miley's place on trumpet. At first everyone thought Cootie should imitate Miley. Fortunately, Cootie wasn't interested in sounding like anybody else; a trumpet player with a strong high range, Cootie Williams quickly became recognized for his individuality and his own unique "wah-wah" style.

Miley wasn't the only one of Duke's musicians to take part in the wilder side of the Jazz Age. There was a lot of drinking going on, a lot of chasing after the Cotton Club's beautiful dancers, and a lot of partying. Things improved when trumpet player Arthur Whetsel (who was in and out of Duke's band for years) came back into the band in 1928. Whetsel, like Duke, grew up in the Uptown neighborhood of Washington, D.C. He wanted Duke's band to be a credit to the Negro race—that was the way he and Duke were raised. He made sure that everyone's suits were clean and shoes were shined, and that they were on time for shows or else would get fined.

GOLDEN YEARS AT THE COTTON CLUB

During the Cotton Club years, Duke seemed to have a golden touch. The Cotton Club's radio broadcasts gave Duke's recording career a huge boost; he played his new tunes at the club, they were heard on the radio, and then some of them became big-selling records, like "East St. Louis Toodle-O," "Creole Love Call," and "Black and Tan Fantasy."

These records were made for the Victor label, one of the most important jazz record labels at that time. Duke's producers at Victor saw that Duke had a knack for using recording technology that made the band sound as good as possible on records. He experimented with the band's seating arrangement and microphone placement, and was interested in all the latest advances. He pushed the limit of how much music could fit on a 78 rpm, and came out with the first extended-play single back in the early 1930s.

Meanwhile, Ellington's personal life got complicated. His good looks, charm, and growing fame attracted women more than ever. He became involved with a dancer from the Cotton Club and left his wife Edna to move in with her. Remarkably—perhaps because of his close-knit family upbringing—Duke still acted like a family man in some ways. He rented a huge apartment in Sugar Hill, the prettiest part of Harlem, and set it up for his mother Daisy, his sister Ruth, and his son Mercer. He showered Daisy with gifts and fine clothes and sent money to his father, who did not wish to move from Washington, D.C.

He helped support Edna financially, and they never got legally divorced; he provided for her the rest of her life.

Duke coined the best comment about his romantic life, though: "Music Is My Mistress" (this was the title he gave the autobiography he wrote near the end of his life). Music was also his wife, extended family, and social life. Even after the last stragglers left the Cotton Club, Duke stayed to play cards with the manager and owner, who really liked him and protected him from some of the threatening gangsters that came along.

The good life of the Jazz Age came to a screeching halt for many people on October 29, 1929, also known as "Black Tuesday," when the stock market crashed. This event was the spark that ignited the Great Depression, a catastrophic economic downturn that lasted through the mid-1930s. It was widespread; rich people lost their fortunes, middle class people lost what they had worked hard for, and poor people endured even more suffering. Life was especially hard for the great numbers of black Americans who had just begun to get a foothold economically in northern cities.

Yet, during hard times, music often provides an outlet for people—it can be uplifting, distracting, and entertaining. Amazingly, Duke Ellington and his band members worked steadily throughout the worst years of the Depression. Their good fortune was in stark contrast to many of their friends who were having a difficult time just surviving.

One key to Duke's success in the early years of the Depression was that his music was at the tip of a new trend. One of Duke's most popular songs of the early 1930s said it all: "It Don't Mean a Thing (If It Ain't Got That Swing)." A strong rhythmic drive—a forward-moving rhythm called "swing"—was what gave Duke's band its powerful unity. In another four years, swing music would define the era, just as a rock beat or a hip-hop dance beat does today.

DUKE DURING THE DEPRESSION

Remarkably, the entertainment industry did not collapse all at once after Black Tuesday. Duke's success at the Cotton Club gave him and the band many opportunities. In the summer of 1929, they were invited to be part of a new revue by Ziegfeld Follies in New York City, one of the most celebrated theater and vaudeville shows of all time. Duke's band was the first African American band to be part of the Follies, and they got a stunning reception.

One thing kept leading to another. In early 1931, Irving Mills lined up the band's first big tour of northern cities—Chicago, Minneapo-

lis, and Denver, and back through different cities to New York. They were groundbreakers—the first black band to be hired by several national theater chains, smoothing the path for other bands to follow. They put on stage shows with other acts—comedians, singers,

Vocalist Ivie Anderson and Duke Ellington, 1931, shortly after Ivie joined Duke's band. Institute of Jazz Studies

Activity
Design a Band's Look

THE WAY THE big bands looked onstage was a big element of their popularity. Duke always insisted on elegance, and the band always looked great for special occasions. Through the long history of the band, styles changed, and Duke always wanted his men to look up-to-date. They went from tailored dark suits in the 1920s, to white suits in the 1930s, to the sharp looking "zoot" suits of the 1940s. Duke often wore a tuxedo, and for special formal occasions the whole band did. If you were a bandleader of a rock band, a pop group, or a jazz big band, what kind of outfits would you have your musicians wear? Try to create ideas for a bands' look.

YOU'LL NEED
- ♪ Paper
- ♪ Pencils
- ♪ Pictures of musicians from magazines or CD covers
- ♪ Colored pencils or markers
- ♪ Computer (optional)

List the number of people that are in your ideal band, and how many members are male or female. Now answer these basic questions. Do you want your band to look casual or dressed up? Should the musicians be dressed exactly alike, or just have some similar elements of their costumes, like ties, hats, or special accessories? Do your musicians move around a lot onstage?

What is going to look good, but also be comfortable for performing? Now start looking up pictures of some of your favorite bands on CD covers or in magazines. Try to determine what kind of look best suits the music your group plays: wild and crazy, sweet and sentimental, old-fashioned swing, or country music. Then try your hand at sketching a design for at least two members of your band; if you prefer, you can try to design your band's costumes using your computer.

Duke Ellington and His Orchestra, c. 1940.
Institute of Jazz Studies

70

dancers—at big fancy movie theaters in 30 cities. They broke box office records at every stop. Reviewers unanimously called Duke's band "the biggest sensation to hit the city in a theatrical way."

What was their secret?

For one thing, they had great visual appeal. They were all dressed in white suits, Duke himself wore a white tuxedo, and the horn players choreographed their moves so they swung out their horns together or flipped their mutes. They paced their music dramatically, just like at the Cotton Club, building in intensity to their most powerfully swinging tunes.

At the band's first stop in Chicago, Duke hired a full-time female singer, something he'd been thinking about for a while. He heard Ivie Anderson with a noted Chicago bandleader and hired her on the spot. She turned out to be perfect for Duke's band. Anderson was joyful and energetic and had a clear, crisp voice, strong enough to be heard without a microphone. She became a showstopper herself; she'd run out on stage, also dressed all in white, throwing kisses to the crowd and joking with Sonny Greer, the band's perennial showman. She ended up staying with the band for 11 years.

Duke Ellington and His Orchestra became a household name during 1931, thanks to great reviews and local broadcasts of his shows on every stop of this six-week tour. Irving Mills helped strategize to get Duke even more publicity, recordings, and appearances. In 1931, "Mood Indigo," a lovely impressionistic ballad, became Duke's biggest-selling record to date. First titled "Dreamy Blues," it featured the unusual combination of clarinet, trumpet, and trombone, playing very softly and smoothly. Duke wrote it quickly one afternoon to have a new piece to play on the radio that night. The next day, hundreds of letters poured into the radio station requesting to hear it again. Polished up and recorded as "Mood Indigo," it was named Victor's Record of the Month for February 1931.

Suddenly, other labels wanted to record Duke and his band, too. The band made over 160 recordings between 1928 and 1931, and often used pseudonyms to get around their contract with Victor: the Whoopee Makers, the Harlem Footwarmers, and the Jungle Band were all actually Duke Ellington and His Orchestra.

Meanwhile, a technical innovation in the movie industry in the late 1920s also gave Duke and his musicians a lot of exposure. Movies now had sound and musical soundtracks. Producers started making short, dramatic, musical films that were shown before feature films and were a great way for fans to see what a band looked like. Duke's first film of this nature was *Black and Tan*, a 19-minute drama set to Duke's music. Duke plays himself, a hardworking composer and bandleader, who rescues a dancer when she collapses on-

(left to right) Trumpet player Arthur Whetsel, dancer Fredi Washington, and Duke, in Duke's first film, *Black and Tan* (1929). Institute of Jazz Studies

stage, standing up to the villainous nightclub owner. The film was revolutionary in the way it presented black people onscreen in a non-stereotypic way.

Duke got other film offers, too. He and the band had taken leave from the Cotton Club in the fall of 1930 to be part of a Hollywood film called *Check and Double Check*, featuring the comedy team of Amos and Andy, who were big radio stars. Duke and his band were hired to appear in several key scenes, for which they got paid a huge salary (reportedly $5,000 a week for three weeks of filming). Irving Mills insisted that the band travel to Hollywood in two private railroad cars to spare them the humiliation of discrimination on the road in hotels and restaurants.

Check and Double Check was a film version of a radio show featuring the comic mishaps of Amos and Andy, the fictional African American friends from rural Georgia who came to live in Harlem. The actors (who were also the show's creators) were white, but many of their fans believed that they were black. For the movie, Amos and Andy appeared in dark makeup, as did some of the other minor characters. Meanwhile, the director insisted that two of Duke's light-skinned musicians wear dark makeup so they would not appear to be white. The film expressed many stereotypes of the time. For instance, the white characters lived in fancy mansions; many of the black characters were poor and illiterate. Duke and his musicians were about the only believable characters in the movie, and they just played themselves—a working band.

Like his mother had always told him, Duke was blessed. During the depths of the Depression, Duke was earning his highest fees ever, and he and the band traveled in their own Pullman railroad cars from New York to Hollywood and back.

After being in Hollywood, Duke and the band had returned to the Cotton Club triumphantly, resuming their place as Harlem's premiere band, even though most of the citizens of Harlem couldn't come hear them there. As things turned out, by the spring of 1931, the band's long stay at the Cotton Club was over. Other more tempting offers lured Duke Ellington and His Orchestra away.

Altogether, Duke and the band had been at the Cotton Club for a total of 38 months—a little over three years. In those years Duke had become a huge star, with one of the best-paid bands in the country. They'd made three movies and almost 200 recordings, many of which were big hits, such as "Rockin' in Rhythm," "Mood Indigo," and "Ol' Man Blues." Through the media of records, radio, and film, Duke

ELLINGTON'S BAND IN THE MOVIES

Check and Double Check was not the blockbuster everyone hoped it would be. But Duke Ellington and the band received a lot of publicity and appeared in several other movies during the 1930s and 1940s. They played themselves (again) in two other Hollywood films, *Belle of the Nineties* and *Murder at the Vanities*, and were also featured in a nine-minute drama titled *Symphony in Black*, with an ambitious Ellington score. The star of *Belle of the Nineties* was the great comedienne Mae West, who insisted that Duke and his band appear in the film. Duke's few lines in the movie were mere small talk, but this was the first time onscreen that a black character exchanged dialogue with a white actress.

Symphony in Black was a different story altogether. A groundbreaking film, it was more in tune with Duke's aspirations as a serious composer. *Symphony in Black*, subtitled *A Rhapsody of Negro Life*, painted a portrait of African American life in ways that no one had accomplished before in music or film. The movie has four brief episodes: a hard-labor scene; a love triangle that features a young Billie Holiday (years before she became famous); a church scene; and "Harlem Rhythm," a nightclub scene with "Snake Hips" Tucker and the Cotton Club Dancers. The film score points toward the larger compositions Duke would soon set himself to work on, telling a far larger story than his three-minute hit records.

had attracted a huge audience, both black and white. Even then Duke's music went beyond any strict categories; it was the ultimate combination of swinging jazz, dance music, and personal expression. ∾

6

"IT DON'T MEAN A THING"—DUKE IN THE SWING ERA

Duke's rise to stardom had taken place in the midst of an economic depression of unprecedented scope. Signs of hardship and unemployment were visible everywhere. Duke's beloved Harlem had gone from the land of promise to a slum with many social problems, as did other African American communities in big cities.

The entertainment industry as a whole was now crumbling, and thousands of musicians were out of work. Small local dance bands had trouble finding jobs, and many movie theaters and dance halls closed for lack of business. Record sales, which in 1929 had reached an all-time high of 75 million, fell to 6 million in 1933. Ellington, one of Victor's most successful recording artists, was asked to cut back dramatically on the number of records he made. People didn't have money to spend on records, so radio became the "poor man's phonograph." As a result, entertainment shows on radio came into their own during the 1930s and surpassed phonograph records in popularity, influence, and variety.

Yet Duke was still a huge success, and Duke Ellington and His Famous Orchestra (as they were now called) were trailblazers. They went on almost back-to-back national tours in the spring and summer of 1931, crisscrossing the country. They continued to perform at the big-city theaters and movie palaces that were still in business, many of which had never hired black performers before. They broke box office records everywhere they went, and Duke received at least 200 fan letters a day. After the tours were over they returned to New York City, the band's home base, but from then on they played there only for short periods. They were now a headlining act, and opportunities kept coming.

At the same time that Duke's national fame grew, his compositions were getting attention from serious modern composers. In 1932, the noted composer Percy Grainger invited Duke to talk to his students at New York University. He received rave reviews from music critics who usually wrote about classical music. In

Poster for a concert.
Institute of Jazz Studies

1933, Duke was presented an award for "Best Composition" by the New York School of Music for his extended composition *Creole Rhapsody,* chosen because it "portrayed the Negro life as no other piece had."

Because Duke now spent so much time traveling, he learned to compose almost anywhere—on buses, cars, trains, and, in later years, on planes. He was very self-disciplined, and got by on very little sleep. He could get inspired by almost anything—a place, a color, a story he'd heard. There are at least five Ellington compositions inspired by Harlem: "Jungle Nights in Harlem," "Harlem River Quiver," "Harlem Air Shaft," "Drop Me Off in Harlem," and a full suite called *Harlem.* Duke was also inspired by the sounds of his musicians; their instrumental "voices" were so intertwined with the way he composed that he wrote their names on the parts; for example, the saxophone part was "For Harry," not "Baritone sax," or "Third saxophone," etc. Some were mini-jazz concertos: *Concerto for Cootie* was for trumpet player Cootie Williams, *Clarinet's Lament* was for clarinetist Barney Bigard, and so forth.

In the mid-1930s, *Reminiscing in Tempo* and the music for the film *Symphony in Black* marked Duke's first full-scale efforts as a serious composer. Both compositions were dramas expressed through instrumental music. One critic called these pieces "a gigantic for-

ward stride, not only in jazz, but in the history of black music in America."

Remarkably, Ellington and his band managed to keep working and touring through the worst years of the Depression. In 1933, the rock-bottom year, Ellington and the band made a triumphant comeback at the Cotton Club. Then a few months later, they boarded the S.S. *Olympic,* an ocean liner, for their very first trip abroad to Europe.

Duke, his musicians, a few dancers, and other members of their stage show troupe set sail from New York City on June 2, 1933, and arrived in England a week later. For two weeks they played to sold-out houses in London at the famous Palladium Theater, where once again they broke all box office records. The band was stunned by thunderous applause that lasted for over 10 minutes! The British newspapers all proclaimed that Duke Ellington and His Orchestra were the most successful American cultural attraction that ever performed in Great Britain.

Duke and the band toured Britain and Scotland for six weeks, sometimes playing two or more shows a day. Then they went on to Holland and Paris. Everywhere they went Duke and the band were treated like

Label for "Reminiscing in Tempo," recorded in 1937.
Institute of Jazz Studies

Think Like a Composer— What Inspires You?

DUKE ELLINGTON FOUND inspiration in many things for his compositions: street sounds, trains, traveling to foreign countries. Several of his compositions were either inspired by color or expressed color in sound, especially shades of blue: among the most well-known are "Mood Indigo," "Blue Serge," and "Diminuendo and Crescendo in Blue." Other kinds of artists do that as well. Pablo Picasso went through a period called his "Blue Period," in which all his paintings had a deep blue background, and the figures in them had a bluish tint to their skin. Use this idea for inspiration and create a musical composition. You can compose your piece using whatever musical instruments you have at home, like a piano, electronic keyboard or guitar, or make up a song to sing.

YOU'LL NEED

♪ Musical instrument, such as xylophone, piano, electronic keyboard, or guitar, or one of the instruments you can make in this book

♪ Pencil
♪ Music paper
♪ Tape recorder (optional)

Pick out your favorite color or your favorite season as a way to inspire you to create a song or short musical composition. For example, what kinds of musical qualities express a deep blue color? Does your color make you feel happy, sad, or thoughtful? Does it make you think of fast or slow things? What feeling best suits that color? Make up a melody that is between 8 and 16 measures long, or that follows the 12-bar blues form. You can use 4-measure phrases that repeat, too. Use an instrument to compose your melody, like a piano or keyboard, or sing it. Once you have the melody firmly in your mind, hum it, sing it, or play it several times. If you know musical notation, try to write it out. If not, use a tape recorder and record your composition. Then try to graph out your composition on music paper: include how many measures it is, and how many beats are in each measure. What is the shape of the melody? What other instruments could be added to express the mood of your composition?

celebrities. They were invited to perform at parties thrown by elite British society. At one famous party, the Prince of Wales even sat in on drums. Duke and the band made headlines every day of their tour.

More significantly, Duke and his musicians couldn't believe how seriously Europeans took their music. They were treated like artists— not just entertainers. One newspaper called Duke "the first composer of uncommon merit, probably the first composer of real character to come out of America."

Harry Carney, the baritone saxophonist, said:

We were greeted by so many people who knew so much about the band that we were amazed. We couldn't understand how people in Europe, who heard us only through the medium of records, could know so much about us. They'd ask us who took which solo on this or that tune, and we had to sharpen up so we could answer intelligently.

"The main thing I got in Europe was *spirit*," Duke wrote later on. "That kind of thing gives you the courage to go on. If they think I'm *that* important, and then maybe I have kind of said something, maybe our music does mean something."

On August 1, 1933, the band gave a spectacular farewell concert in Paris, and two days later set sail for home on the ocean liner *Majestic*. They hardly had a chance to unpack before they were back on the road for a week in Boston, and then their annual summer dance-band tour of New England.

HOME ON THE ROAD

 When the band settled back home in New York that fall, Duke was finally feeling the pinch of the Depression, especially since he now had a bigger payroll—the band had grown to 15 members. Irving Mills promised Duke good money if Duke and the band would tour big cities in the Southern states, which Duke had so far refused to do. Duke was fearful of the kind of racial incidents he'd heard about from other black bandleaders, especially from Cab Calloway, the leader of the first black big band to tour the South. Cab's pianist described the situation like this: "They've got us coming and leaving from the backs of theaters, dressing in toilets, and eating while we sit on potato sacks." Cab's musicians had to find rooms in homes in black neighborhoods, since the hotels refused to take black patrons.

Mills promised Duke to send aides in advance to set up good publicity and stake out decent places to stay. Duke finally agreed, and he and the band left for a 12-week tour of the South and Southwest, starting in Dallas and working their way back through Oklahoma, on to New Orleans, and up through Alabama and Georgia. Again, Duke and the band were trailblazers. This was the first time a Southern theater chain hired a black band to perform for a stage show, and Duke and the band took Dallas by storm. The Majestic Theater in Dallas sold a record-breaking number of seats the week that Duke and the band were there. They played five shows a day, broke all attendance records, and made $22,000!

Even so, this trip was different for Duke and his men, most of whom had never experienced such blatant racism or enforced segregation. There were times when elevator operators in fancy hotels refused to take them and they had to ride the freight elevator, despite Duke's fame. At a ballroom in Dallas, one dance was held for whites and another for blacks, at which white spectators had reserved seats. In some theaters, black people were only permitted to hear the band if they sat way up in the second balcony and entered and exited through a "colored only" door. In Atlanta, the band played at the city auditorium where the black audience had to stand in the back, while only the white people sat in the seats. Clarinetist Barney Bigard said that at several

"What I am trying to get across is that music for me is a language. It expresses more than just sound. I often think of tones as colors or memories, and all that helps in composing."

dance halls on their trip, "they always had to have four cops stationed at each corner of the place so that the local people wouldn't get any ideas." There were never violent incidents, but there was often tension.

Even from a professional standpoint, Duke faced hurdles despite his fame. Duke and the band broadcast live on the radio at almost every stop on their tour, but Duke never got his own nationally sponsored radio show like prominent white bandleaders did.

"That was a very, very busy time, and there were probably more jazz musicians working then than ever before or since. The audience expanded overnight. . . . It was a dancing time and there were occasions when they turned more people away from the Savoy Ballroom than they had inside."

Duke's philosophy was to always rise above discrimination, no matter how exasperating the circumstances. He refused to feel humiliated, and always kept cool in tense situations. He would say "I'm not going to allow that to set me aside and distract me. That's their problem, not my problem." He also started refusing jobs where he and his men could not be guaranteed decent treatment.

Nonetheless, everyone was relieved when they returned to Chicago after eight weeks. Sonny Greer said, "Man, we were so happy to get back up North. I'd never been South before. When we got off the train in Chicago I wanted to kneel and kiss the ground."

Duke and the band returned to tour the South the following year, but they took some matters into their own hands. Irving Mills hired three private railroad cars—two sleeping cars and a baggage car. Sometimes they even had a dining car. This was how the band traveled from 1934 to 1936 and avoided the worst aspects of touring—finding accommodations on the road, especially in the South. Duke enjoyed turning the tables on people in this regard. He said: "We commanded respect. We parked those cars in each railroad station and we lived in them. . . . The natives would come by and they would say, 'What on earth is that?' And we would say, 'That's the way the President travels.'"

Make Two Percussion Instruments

SONNY GREER, Duke Ellington's longtime drummer, was a full-scale percussionist as well as a drummer. He had not only a drum kit but also a full assortment of chimes, bells, gongs, whistles, and shakers. Today, most jazz and rock 'n' roll drummers have something similar: a standard drum kit—bass drum, a snare drum, several cymbals, and tom toms—plus a variety of percussion instruments. Percussion instruments are used to keep the beat, and also to add color and texture to a composition. Here are instructions for two easy percussion instruments, a rain stick and a shaker. Try your hand at making them and playing them!

MAKE A RAIN STICK

YOU'LL NEED

♪ Hammer
♪ ½ pound of 1½-inch nails
♪ Mailing tube, 1½ inches diameter, 36 inches long
♪ Covers for the ends of the tube (you can use heavy cardboard if the tube does not come with covers)
♪ 1 cup rice, dry beans, small pebbles, or macaroni—anything that will produce a soft rattling sound when moving through the tube

♪ Measuring cup
♪ Wide-mouth funnel
♪ Glue
♪ Colored paper
♪ Poster paint
♪ Paint brushes
♪ Crepe-paper streamers (optional)
♪ Colored electrical tape

1. Carefully hammer the nails along the length of the tube. Try to drive the nails straight through, so the ends of the nails don't poke out the other side (if this happens, you can just push the nails back out and adjust the angle). Look down the tube and see what kind of maze you have created for the rice, beans, or other materials to slide through when you are done.

2. When you are finished hammering in the nails, seal up one end of the tube. Use the stopper the tube came with, or cut a circle of heavy cardboard to fit over the end of the tube, then tape over it to seal that end.

3. Experiment with a small amount of material to create the sound you like the best. Pour in ½ cup rice, beans, macaroni, or other similar substance. You can also try using a combination of smaller and larger beans and grains. Put your hand over the open end, and slowly tip the rain stick up and down to hear the results.

4. Pour a total of one cup of rice, beans, or your combination through the funnel into the tube. Seal up the open end with the other stopper, or

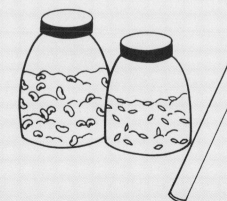

continued...

Make Two Percussion Instruments, *continued*

make the second stopper out of cardboard and tape (as in step 2) to seal up the rain stick.

5. The final step is decorating. Create a pattern with the colored electrical tape, glue on strips of colored paper, or paint a colorful pattern. You can even add crepe-paper streamers to the ends.

6. To play the instrument, slowly tip one end of the rain stick up, then reverse sides. You will get a bewitching, soothing sound, like falling water.

MAKE A SHAKER

You can make a shorter, wider version of the rain stick, which will be more like a maraca or shaker. The short, wider tube will allow the rice, beans, or other material to pass through it more quickly, producing a larger sound. Use a tube with a 3-inch diameter, about 8 inches long. Follow the steps for making a rain stick, except omit hammering in nails. To play this instrument, shake up and down to the beat.

By 1936, the economy finally started sputtering back to life, though full economic recovery would take years. The upturn helped reenergize the entertainment world. Dance bands were back in business, thanks to the huge popularity of clarinetist Benny Goodman's big band, which had swept the country up in a swing fever in the late summer of 1935, officially launching the swing era.

In the 1930s and even on through World War II, the big bands were the rock bands of the swing era, and inspired fierce loyalty among fans. Teenagers and college kids flocked to dances and invented acrobatic steps and routines. The bands' fabulous music was only part of what drew thousands of people to the Savoy Ballroom in Harlem, or the Palomar in Los Angeles: so did their sharp suits and shining horns.

Young bandleaders like Benny Goodman looked to Duke and other pioneer swing bandleaders such as Fletcher Henderson and Chick Webb, whose great big band was the heart of the famed Savoy Ballroom, Harlem's "Home of Happy Feet." A whole new crop of big bands—black and white—sprang up. Jimmie Lunceford's band, with their choreographed movements and powerful arrangements—was Duke's biggest rival and a hit on the college circuit. The world of big bands was like major-league sports: it was big news when a hot trumpet player joined a rival band. These were the years when jazz-based dance music and popular music were one and the same.

The downside of the swing era was that the big dance bands became a big business (also like major league sports). The stakes were high, the competition fierce, and a lot of imitators were out there. During the mid-to-late 1930s, the bands of Benny Goodman and trombonist Tommy Dorsey started to zoom past Duke's in terms of popularity polls, and so did their performance fees. Typically, Duke remained unruffled by all the new competition. He just said, "Jazz is music, swing is business."

FRIENDLY RIVALS—TOP BIG BANDS OF THE ERA

By the late 1930s, Duke Ellington's band had plenty of competition. The bands led by Benny Goodman and Count Basie were two of his biggest rivals, and there were legendary "battles of the bands" between them—fabulous nights to remember at Harlem's Savoy Ballroom and other places. But all three leaders had the utmost respect for each other's music, and there was a lot of mutual admiration among their musicians.

Clarinetist **Benny Goodman** was born in Chicago in 1909, picked up the clarinet at age 11, and was working professionally when he was 13. After playing in several dance bands Goodman, inspired by the music of Fletcher Hen-derson and Duke Ellington, formed his own big band in New York City. The band scuffled along for a while and was almost ready to break up when they decided to play one of their hottest jazz arrangements at a dance in California. The teenage crowd went crazy. A broadcast caught the excitement and was heard across the country. Almost overnight, Benny Goodman was hailed as the "King of Swing," and he hired Fletcher Hender-son to write some of his arrangements, most notably "Sing, Sing, Sing."

continued...

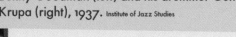

Benny Goodman (left) and his drummer Gene Krupa (right), 1937. Institute of Jazz Studies

83

William "Count" Basie was born in 1904 in New Jersey, and died in 1984. He started making his living as a pianist with traveling vaudeville shows. In the late 1920s, he got stranded in Kansas City, when that city was a melting pot for a bluesy riff-based jazz style. After playing with the best bands in town, he took over the leadership of a band that played at a small club called the Reno Club. The band's radio broadcasts caught the ear of John Hammond, then Benny Goodman's manager, who brought Basie's band to New York. Two years later, they were world famous and become as influential in their style as Duke was with his. The band's most popular songs were "One O'Clock Jump" and "Jumpin' at the Woodside."

Count Basie and His Orchestra, another great band of the swing era.
Institute of Jazz Studies

Duke's personal life was as full of highs and lows as the music business during the 1930s, though he kept his problems closely guarded from the public and even from his friends. In the fall of 1933, a few weeks after the band returned from Europe, Duke's mother, Daisy, became very ill. By the next year, she was diagnosed with cancer. She was eventually sent for treatment to a research hospital in Detroit, where she died on May 27, 1935, with Duke and other loved ones at her side. Just a year and a half later his father became very ill. James Edward Ellington was hospitalized in New York City for several months; Duke was at his side, too, when he died October 28, 1937.

Daisy's death left Duke extremely depressed. He had always been completely devoted to her. When she came to live in New York City, he showered her with lavish gifts, and saw to her every need. Her illness and death were a huge loss for him. It was hard for him to focus on composing and keep up the nonstop creative pace he'd kept up for years, even though he and the band were as busy as ever.

Unfortunately, Duke was in a lot of debt due to his parents' medical bills, long hospital stays, and funeral expenses. Duke's strong work ethic finally pulled him out of his slump. He knew he had to stay creative and keep moving forward for the band to survive financially. Out of necessity Duke accepted more one-night jobs. When one band member complained about all the traveling, Duke said, "As long as this [railroad] car is rolling I am not losing any money."

A few months after Daisy's death, Duke wrote *Reminiscing in Tempo*, one of his most ambitious pieces to date, in memory of her. The recording of this piece got such great reviews that Duke became recharged about composing again.

In December 1937, Duke and the band celebrated the 10th anniversary of their debut at the Cotton Club, the job that had brought Duke such tremendous fame. "The Duke is still King" proclaimed ads in music magazines. By this time, Duke was a respected figure. *Life* magazine named Ellington as one of the "Twenty Most Prominent Negroes" in the country. He had become a spokesman for black Americans because he was so well-known, but in truth he spoke more through his music than in any other way. Drummer Sonny Greer explained, "All through the years, Duke has been deeply concerned about his race and its problems. But the man never makes it a great point of his interest; he's too subtle for that. He composes works like *Black, Brown and Beige, Deep South Suite,* and *Harlem*—leaving it to the people to find and interpret his thoughts for them."

Duke could hardly rest on his fame. Keeping his band employed and happy was like supporting a huge extended family, or running a company. During the swing era, competition for the best-paying jobs, radio spots, and record contracts was fierce. At the same time, Duke wanted to write larger works, compositions that would go beyond the three-minute pop songs that he was churning out once again.

The late 1930s were years of change for Duke in other ways, too. His romantic life affected his immediate family. Duke fell in love again, this time with Beatrice Evie Ellis, a hostess from the "downtown Cotton Club." When Duke and Evie set up household together, Duke helped his sister, Ruth, and son, Mercer, then both in their early 20s, move to a large new apartment that he also considered home base. Ruth was a student at Columbia University. Mercer, who played trumpet and was starting to write music, too, was studying at Juilliard, a music conservatory. But he often traveled with the band and helped out with instruments and equipment.

Another person who became part of Duke's inner circle in the late 1930s was a talented young composer named Billy Strayhorn. In December 1938, Strayhorn, a great fan of Ellington's music, plucked up his courage and went to introduce himself to Duke backstage after a concert in his hometown, Pittsburgh, Pennsylvania. Strayhorn had attended a music

Billy Strayhorn in Pittsburgh.
Courtesy David Hajdu

conservatory there after high school. He went backstage after the show, and Duke invited him to play for him. Strayhorn played some of Duke's own songs, and a few of his own. Duke was clearly impressed, and said, "Why young man, I'm going to bring you to New York, and you will be my lyric writer."

This sounded like an empty promise, but a month later, Strayhorn, then 23 years old, came to New York. Ruth and Mercer were close in age to Billy and liked him right away; they invited him to stay with them after he'd spent a couple of sleepless nights at the nearby YMCA. He quickly became a member of Duke's family and a favorite among Duke's musicians. For a while, it was unclear whether Duke was giving Strayhorn a formal job, or exactly what he would be doing for the Ellington band. Duke was touring a lot and getting ready to tour Europe for the second time. So Strayhorn worked on his own compositions and explored the city, soaking up all kinds of music and culture. Even with the uncertainty, Billy Strayhorn knew he had made the right move.

In March 1939, Duke and the band sailed to Europe. During this trip, they had an even more demanding schedule than their first European tour; they played 29 concerts in 24 days. They were greeted with an uproarious welcome when the ship arrived at the dock in Le Havre, France. Trumpet player

Rex Stewart, who had joined the band in 1934, said, "There were a lot of people from all over France and Europe there to welcome us ... who all greeted us with such absolute adoration and genuine joy that, for the first time in my life, I had the feeling of being accepted as an artist, a gentleman, and a member of the human race."

This time, Duke and the band performed only in concert settings and were astonished by the level of appreciation of their music. The formal concert settings, lavish printed programs, and intelligently written reviews all reaffirmed Duke's perception of himself as a serious artist and composer. "The audiences acted as though they were at a symphony concert," said trombonist Lawrence Brown.

But this time the atmosphere in Europe was quite different. Hitler's Nazi forces were already occupying other countries, and the threat of war hung over every place the band visited. As they travelled by train they sometimes saw German machine gun posts in haystacks and ditches. There were German soldiers and Nazi SS guards at the ferry landing in Hamburg, Germany, and the band, en route to Sweden, was screened by SS guards. Clarinetist Barney Bigard never forgot that: "The SS border guards looked like Satan himself, like they would eat you up." Duke said they were scared to death.

Duke and his musicians were relieved to get to Stockholm, Sweden, where a huge crowd welcomed them at the train station. Duke celebrated his 40th birthday there. He was awakened by a 16-piece Swedish band serenading him, and many festivities had been planned for him. Many Swedes at Duke's concerts were hearing jazz for the first time and responded to the band with complete adoration. Duke was overwhelmed by the Swedish people's lavish hospitality; while still there, he composed *Serenade to Sweden* to thank them.

Two months later, Duke and his musicians sailed home on the *Ile de France*. The ship was filled with regular passengers, but also with many refugees fleeing Hitler, and Americans returning home who had been living abroad. All that people talked about was the impending war and how relieved they were to get out of Europe. "I was never so glad to see that old Statue of Liberty," said Barney Bigard. ∾

7

TAKE THE "A" TRAIN

After Duke and his band returned from their second tour of Europe, they entered a dizzying creative period, coming up with new material and performing at a high level. Their energy, unity, and unique sound made them a huge attraction everywhere, and a standout among the other top bands. In the early 1940s, still peak years of the swing era, Duke's band turned out a string of hit records: "Koko," "Take the 'A' Train," "Jack the Bear," "Cotton Tail," and many others. You can still hear the band's excitement and energy on their recordings from these years.

Much of the magic in the band at that time was due to the chemistry of the group. Some of the musicians had been with the band for well over a decade. By 1940, for instance, drummer Sonny Greer had been with Duke for 17 years, guitarist Fred Guy for 15, and several of the best horn players—Johnny Hodges, Harry Carney, Barney Bigard, Cootie Williams, and Juan Tizol—between 10 and 14 years.

The newcomers—composer-arranger Billy Strayhorn, saxophonist Ben Webster, and bassist Jimmie Blanton—gave the band a boost of inspiration and a more contemporary sound. When Duke returned from Europe, he asked Strayhorn to do the band's vocal arrangements and to help out with other material as well. Ben Webster was already considered a giant on tenor saxophone, now an important jazz instrument. His earthy style and big sound were imitated by everyone. The 20-year-old bassist Jimmie Blanton came to Duke's attention while the band was on tour in St. Louis. Duke went to hear him play, and, like Ivie Anderson, Blanton impressed Duke so much that he hired Blanton on the spot. Blanton was the first modern-sounding bass player Duke's band ever had. He gave the entire band a lift with his fluid style of playing swing; the music leapt and danced in his hands.

Another big change at this time was nonmusical, but very significant. Duke formally broke off relations with his longtime manager, Irving Mills. This was something he'd been thinking about doing for a while. Mills had been spending more and more time looking out for his other clients and the two small recording companies he'd started; Duke felt that Mills was not paying as much attention to the band as he should.

There were other reasons, too. For years, Mills had capitalized on Duke's talents, and even signed on to some of Duke's tunes as co-composer, without really being a collaborator. Unfortunately, that was what many song publishers did, allowing them to earn royalties, too, when a song became successful. Mills always pressured Duke to keep pumping out new pop songs, which were then published by Mills's publishing company and recorded by his record company. Mills did not encourage Duke to write the longer, serious compositions that Duke was interested in because they didn't seem "hit-worthy." But Duke was always a gentleman and diplomatic; he publicly acknowledged the good things Mills had helped him accomplish in 13 years. After all, Mills was Duke's manager when no one had ever heard of Duke Ellington and His Washingtonians.

Duke felt free after his break with Mills and put new business relationships in place immediately. He signed on with the prominent

Rhythm Exploration—Learn to Read Drum Notation

SONNY GREER, LIKE the other members of Duke's band, knew all his parts from memory. But there is no question that his notated part, on many of the band's arrangements, was very specific. In the big band era, drummers had written parts, just like all the members of the band. The drummer's part is a representation of the musical arrangement, with drum notation (not quite the same as musical notes). The drummer's part indicates the number of measures; what sections repeat; when the band is playing altogether or when a soloist is featured. It also indicates dynamics—when the music should be loud or soft—and important instructions, such as a big cymbal crash or drum roll. Try this activity to learn about basic drum notation; then see if you can notate a four-bar drum pattern.

YOU'LL NEED

♪ 2 drumsticks or wooden dowels
♪ Block of wood, approximately 2 x 4 x 8 inches
♪ Coffee can or metal pot
♪ Pencil
♪ Music paper

Look at the drum key and musical examples at right. See how the notes and cross marks represent which parts of the drum kit to play (the bass drum, snare, hi-hat, cymbal). Then count out the musical example as indicated, in 4/4 time (that means there will be four beats to one measure, and the quarter note gets one beat); repeat this example until you are comfortable. Now try the example with your sticks and drum kit. Use the block of wood for your drum and the coffee can for your hi-hat and cymbal. See if you can coordinate the sounds and keep a steady beat. Then, notate your own four-bar drum part, using a combination of note values and rests. See what

it sounds like. Does it sound like a rock rhythm, or maybe a swing rhythm?

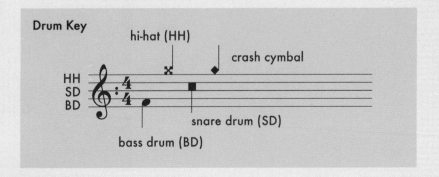

William Morris Agency for booking the band, and the music publisher Jack Robbins. He reestablished a recording contract with RCA Victor, still regarded as the best record label for jazz and big band music. The record label valued Duke's fame and prestige, as well as all his hit records. His new contract made Duke's band the only black band on the label's highest-price Victor label. RCA Victor had another label called Bluebird that recorded other great jazz artists of the day, black and white.

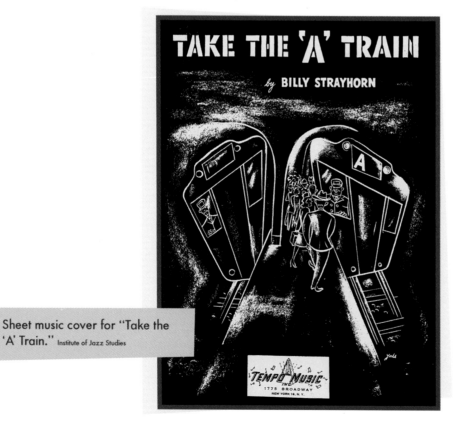

The Ellington Orchestra's leap into creative high gear could not have occurred at a better time. The economy was recovering. Once again, people had enough extra money for entertainment and leisure activities: going to dances and concerts and buying records. Duke's band members were among the best musicians on their instruments in the whole country, and the band was far more adventurous than the other big bands. On top of that, the band's original material made them a standout.

Billy Strayhorn quickly became more and more valuable to Duke as an arranger and composer. Strayhorn had considerable training in classical music and quickly grasped Duke's musical language, working methods, and techniques. Many admirers commented that it was hard to tell where Duke's writing ended and Strayhorn's began.

Strayhorn had access to all of Duke's scores and studied them intently. He once said:

Ellington plays the piano, but his real instrument is the band. Each member of his band is to him a distinctive tone color and set of emotions, which he mixes with others equally distinctive to produce a third thing, which I like to call "Ellington effect." Sometimes the mixing happens on paper and frequently right on the bandstand. I have often seen him exchange parts in the middle of a piece because the man and the part weren't the same character.

Strayhorn wrote several tunes for the band in the winter of 1941, but it wasn't just because he had a creative burst of energy. There was a crisis in the music industry. Starting on New Year's Day, 1941, the American Society of Composers, Authors and Publishers (ASCAP), of which Duke was a member, had banned radio stations from playing music by ASCAP members. The organization wanted higher fees from radio broadcasters for music licensed from ASCAP. Right at that time, Duke and the band were scheduled to play for three weeks at a big nightclub in Los Angeles. Since all Duke's nightclub shows were to be broadcast, he immediately needed a new stockpile of music. He pressed his son Mercer, Billy Strayhorn, and Juan Tizol (the trombonist, who had already done some writing for the band) into churning out new tunes as quickly as possible. Mercer, now almost 22 years old, had tried leading his own band the year before, but it didn't work out. He had also been trying to convince Duke to play his tunes. Mercer jumped at this chance, just like Duke did when he was starting out. For three weeks, Mercer and Billy spent all their waking hours composing.

Mercer explained:

Strayhorn and I got this break at the same time. Overnight, literally, we got a chance to write a whole new book for the band. It could have taken us 20 years to get the old man to make room for that much of our music, but all of a sudden we had this freak opportunity. We were sharing the same room and we had all this work to do. . . . At one point [Strayhorn] was having some sort of trouble and I pulled a piece out of the garbage. I said, "What's wrong with this?" . . . It was "A Train." . . . I flattened it out anyway and put it in a pile with the rest of the stuff.

"Take the 'A' Train" was recorded in February 1941 and was an immediate hit. It quickly became the band's theme song and is an Ellington emblem to this day. One of Mercer's tunes, "Things Ain't What They Used To Be," was also a big hit. These successes inspired Ellington to form his own music publishing company, Tempo Music. Tempo published all of the new material, and every song benefited Duke and the composers directly because they received full royalties for sales of sheet music and recordings. Even so, no matter who was the main composer of a song, Duke had his hand in it: he might alter the melody a bit, or the chord structure or harmony; he refined arrangements continually. Collaboration had always been a major part of Duke's composing and arranging style with his band members. Now Billy Strayhorn was part of that process, too, and would take on more and more of the writing.

JUMP FOR JOY

Duke and the band ended up remaining in Los Angeles for a few months in 1941, and Duke was befriended by several film writers and intellectuals. Some of them were comedy writers who also thought about social issues such as racial and economic inequality. Duke and his new friends decided to put together an all-black musical from the perspective of black people looking irreverently at whites. The resulting show was called *Jump for Joy,* a revue of about 40 songs and skits that poked fun at racial stereotypes, especially those common in Hollywood movies and Broadway shows. For instance, the finale of the first Act was a skit called "Uncle Tom's Cabin Is a Drive-in Now." The writers and cast spent hours together after every performance to talk about what worked and what didn't, what could be funnier, and what might be too insulting.

Jump for Joy opened at the Mayan Theater in Los Angeles on July 10, 1941, and played for three months to sold-out houses. The show starred Dorothy Dandridge, a famous African American actress and singer, the Ellington singers Ivie Anderson and Herb Jeffries, and featured other Hollywood comedians and actors. Even though the show was a hit in Los Angeles, it was hard to secure enough money to produce it in New York City, which Duke would have loved to do. Nonetheless, Duke took a lot of pride in *Jump for Joy.* This experience paved the way for other ambitious works he had been thinking about creating that would express black life in America through a musical canvas.

Mercer Ellington and Billy Strayhorn helped write many of the songs for *Jump for Joy,* continuing to prove themselves. Several songs from the show—"Rocks in My Bed," "Blip-blip," and "Just Squeeze Me"—were made into "soundies" (three-minute musical films that were an early version of music videos). After the show closed in late September 1941, the band was still based in Los Angeles and resumed active touring on the West Coast.

Then tragedy struck. The bassist Jimmie Blanton had been feeling run-down for months. He was diagnosed with advanced tuberculosis and immediately hospitalized. This was a terrible blow for the young, gifted musician, who didn't even smoke or drink like many of the elder members of Ellington's band did. Duke and the other band members were heartbroken about leaving him at a hospital, far from his home and family in the Midwest. Duke did everything he could to make sure Blanton was getting the right care, but Blanton died later that fall.

A WORLD AT WAR

On December 7, 1941, while the band was on tour in the Pacific Northwest, tragedy struck again—this time on a global scale—when the Japanese bombed Pearl Harbor in Hawaii. President Franklin D. Roosevelt immediately declared war on Japan, and America entered World War II, forging bonds with the Allied forces in Europe and in the Far East.

These events affected all aspects of life in the United States, even though the battlefields were thousands of miles away. Duke and most of his musicians were too old to be drafted, but they were directly affected by the war effort, as were other big band musicians. The armed forces commandeered all available forms of transportation and resources to get the troops to training camps and abroad. Traveling for everyone else became restrictive due to gas ra-

tioning and tire shortages. The days of Duke's private railroad cars were over.

The general upheaval in the country affected individual band members, too. In July 1942, the clarinetist Barney Bigard decided to stay in Los Angeles with his fiancée and settle down. A band member since 1928, Bigard's beautiful sound added a rich color to Duke's palette. It took Duke a while to find a suitable replacement—and then that person got drafted. Ivie Anderson decided she also wanted to settle down in Los Angeles with her new husband. Now 38, she had been a professional singer with Duke for 11 years and wanted to settle down and take better care of her health. Herb Jeffries, Duke's male singer, who like Ivie was a big hit with audiences, decided to stay in California, as did trombonist and composer Juan Tizol.

Several singers came and went after Ivie left, including Betty Roche, Kay Davis, Joya Sherrill, and Al Hibbler. In 1943, Ben Webster, Rex Stewart, and Ray Nance, all key musicians, left to form their own groups, lured by the prospect of bigger money and more of the spotlight. Ben Webster's departure left a huge gap in the saxophone section.

Duke struggled to keep the band going under these adverse circumstances. He managed to recruit some excellent newcomers, including the trumpet player Shorty Baker and

Singer Joya Sherrill with Duke Ellington, mid-1940s. Institute of Jazz Studies

MARY LOU WILLIAMS—ARRANGER, PIANIST, JAZZ PIONEER

Duke Ellington worked with many collaborators among his musicians; in addition to Billy Strayhorn, his trombone player Juan Tizol and clarinetist Barney Bigard added several arrangements and compositions to the band's repertoire. Along with them, Mary Lou Williams (1910–1981), one of the foremost women in jazz, did some arrangements for Duke's band in the mid 1940s. A pianist, arranger, and composer, Williams was raised in Pittsburgh and started her long career as a traveling pianist. Like Count Basie, she ended up in Kansas City, Missouri, during the 1920s, which was then a great city for jazz and dance bands. It was there that she became pianist and arranger for Andy Kirk and His Clouds of Joy. In years to come, Williams wrote arrangements for the top big bands, including Benny Goodman, the Dorsey Brothers, and Louis Armstrong.

Williams married her sweetheart, the trumpet player Shorty Baker, soon after he joined Duke's band in 1942, on his day off. Duke lost no time asking her to write some arrangements for the band, and even though she had so much experience, she was still flattered by the offer. Duke's favorite arrangement of Williams's was a feature for her high-note trumpet-playing husband, called "Trumpets No End," a takeoff of "Blue Skies" by Irving Berlin. According to Al Hibbler, one of Duke's main vocalists when Mary Lou Williams was with the band, all of Duke's musicians loved what she did.

Institute of Jazz Studies

clarinetist Jimmy Hamilton in 1943. But soon there was another music industry crisis. Just a few months after the ASCAP broadcasting ban was resolved, the head of the Musicians' Union called for a recording ban by union members. He thought that a popular new music technology—the jukebox!—was causing many musicians to lose their jobs performing in cafés, restaurants, and the like; he wanted the record companies to compensate his union members with better fees for recording. The ban, though well-intended, came at a huge cost for Duke. His record sales and royalties for his songs provided a lot of income for him, which helped keep the band intact. The recording ban lasted for two years, which also meant the loss of exposure for Duke's new musicians and his new compositions during World War II.

Yet even with all these obstacles, Duke Ellington and his band managed to work their way through hard times, just as they had worked their way through the Great Depression. They toured almost as much as before, despite the difficulties of traveling. To help the war effort, Duke played concerts to benefit the Red Cross, anti-fascist groups, and for soldiers in training camps around the United States. The band remained one of the most popular bands all through World War II, and were heard live on the radio almost every

PUTTIN' ON THE RITZ—THE ELLINGTON VOCALISTS

In the late 1920s, Duke, like most bandleaders, had no singers on his staff, but once the big band era went into full swing—literally—many bands hired their own vocalists. When Duke heard Ivie Anderson in Chicago in 1931, he hired her on the spot. Ivie stayed with the band for 11 years, the longest of any of Duke's vocalists. She was versatile. She could sing as fine a ballad or blues as anyone, but her best work was on energetic swing tunes. She left the band in 1942, mostly for health reasons.

Ivie's shoes were hard to fill. During the 1940s Duke hired various singers. At one point he used three female singers—Joya Sherrill, Kay Davis, and Marie Ellington (no relation), along with Al Hibbler, the rich-sounding tenor who stayed with Duke for seven years. Their 1945 version of "It Don't Mean a Thing" is the definitive one, in which they sing the tune like a round. Betty Roche was with Duke briefly in the 1940s. She was a great "scat" singer, which is the term for a singer who improvises like a jazz instrumentalist and sings nonsense syllables instead of words (Ella Fitzgerald was the "first lady of scat").

Duke's vocalists were the icing on the gorgeous layer cake of his band's sound. Over the decades, several star singers wanted to sing with Duke and his band. One can hear the Ellington songbook as interpreted by Frank Sinatra, Bing Crosby, the gospel singer Mahalia Jackson, the blues singer Jimmy Rushing—and the most perfect match of all, Ella Fitzgerald.

Joya Sherrill, Kaye Davis, and Marie Ellington (no relation to Duke), the band's vocalists in the mid-1940s. Institute of Jazz Studies

night. *Saturday Night with the Duke* was a favorite radio series sponsored by the U.S. Treasury Department that broadcast an hour-long show from wherever Duke and the band were performing on Saturday night for almost two years. Duke's work for the Treasury Department made it easier for Duke to get buses for touring. The band also made V-discs (Victory records) that were given out to members of the

armed forces and were treated as prized possessions at home and abroad.

Duke Ellington and His Orchestra continued to be a poll-winner through the war years, and new opportunities kept coming up. In the fall of 1942, Duke and the band were asked to perform in *Cabin in the Sky*, a musical film featuring an all-star African American cast with Ethel Waters, Lena Horne, and Louis Armstrong. It was a loopy comedy, with more stereotypic roles and jokes than *Jump for Joy*.

Duke accepted almost any offer to keep up the band's visibility and morale during the war. A strong, resilient person, his character was consistent in good times and bad: he didn't like arguing with musicians about petty grievances and would avoid it as much as he could. On the road—on trains, in buses, in cars, and later on planes—his habits baffled people who didn't know him. He was a big eater and would eat huge portions at almost every meal, and ask for more. He got by on very little sleep and often didn't go to bed until dawn, but would be hard to awaken from a nap. He loved to dress well and appearance was of utmost importance to him. He turned out hundreds of compositions while traveling, which took an enormous amount of self-discipline.

Even during the war years, Duke's dreams still came to life. For years, he had been working on and off on a major composition that

Album cover for *Black, Brown and Beige*. Institute of Jazz Studies

BEIGE
BLACK and
BROWN

a DUKE ELLINGTON tone parallel to the American Negro

as played by the composer and his Famous Orchestra at his Carnegie Hall concerts would express "the musical evolution of the Negro race." In January 1943, he had an opportunity to present it. Duke and his band were scheduled to perform a benefit concert at Carnegie Hall for the Russian War Relief Fund. Carnegie Hall, home to the world's greatest orchestras and soloists, was exactly the location Duke wanted for the premiere of this piece, titled *Black, Brown and Beige: A Tone Parallel to the History of the Negro in America*. He wanted this new work to be taken as seriously as the symphonies performed in that setting.

Duke worked furiously for six weeks on nothing else but *Black, Brown and Beige*. Like many composers, he recycled some of his ideas, or adjusted melodies or textures that were already part of his "toolbox." This piece was a "programmatic work," meaning Duke composed it with a story in mind: the history of black people in America, from slavery to modern urban life. The suite opens with an instrumental piece, "Work Song" ("the first things the Black man did in America was WORK"); followed by a gospel song called "Come Sunday." Duke was still finishing some details until the night before the concert. It was his most ambitious work to date.

During the weeks leading up to this event, the newspapers and magazines were full of publicity: a concert work by Duke Ellington to be premiered at the most legendary concert

THE CARNEGIE HALL CONCERTS

Less than a year after Duke's Carnegie Hall debut, he decided to do another Carnegie Hall concert, and to have another work ready to premiere. On December 11, 1943, the band performed *New World A-Comin'*. This piece told the musical story of the "new world as a place in the distant future where there would be no war, no greed, no categorization, no nonbelievers, where love was unconditional, and no pronoun was good enough for God."

Carnegie Hall was sold out for this concert, and Duke decided to make the Carnegie Hall performances an annual event. He and the band presented six additional Carnegie Hall concerts through 1948, and some of them were so popular that he added an extra night.

Ellington's new works typically took the form of "suites," which are sets of five or six short, related musical pieces meant to be performed together. Billy Strayhorn co-composed many of the suites, and works such as *Perfume Suite*, *Deep South Suite*, *The Clothed Woman*, and *Liberian Suite* paved a new direction for jazz in the concert hall. For Duke, they were also musical expressions of the African American experience. He once wrote that "the annual Carnegie Hall concerts were really a series of social-significance thrusts."

A CONCERT
OF
THE MUSIC OF
DUKE ELLINGTON

CELEBRATING HIS 20 YEARS AS AN ORCHESTRA LEADER
AT
CARNEGIE HALL
FEATURING
DUKE ELLINGTON'S FIRST SYMPHONY
SATURDAY EVENING, JANUARY 23, 1943

TICKETS: 55c, 83c, $1.10, $1.65, $2.20, $3.30 (tax incl.)   ALL SEATS RESERVED
TICKETS MAY BE OBTAINED FROM
DUKE ELLINGTON ANNIVERSARY COMMITTEE, 1775 BROADWAY, NEW YORK
RUSSIAN WAR RELIEF, INC., 11 EAST 35TH STREET, NEW YORK
CARNEGIE HALL BOX OFFICE
MAKE CHEQUES PAYABLE TO: RUSSIAN WAR RELIEF, INC.

NET PROCEEDS TO RUSSIAN WAR RELIEF
A MERRY CHRISTMAS   A HAPPY NEW YEAR

Advertisement for Duke's first Carnegie Hall concert, 1943. Courtesy Morris Hodara

Activity

Write Lyrics to an Ellington Tune

DUKE ELLINGTON'S SONGS have a special place in what people call the "great American songbook," alongside songs by George and Ira Gershwin, Cole Porter, and Irving Berlin. Remarkably, Duke Ellington's most famous songs were instrumental compositions first—Duke wrote them for his musicians to play and they did not have any lyrics. But some of Duke's tunes proved to be so popular that Duke knew they would make great songs, so he and his collaborators added lyrics later on; the vocal versions came out on record years later. Some of the most famous examples are "Mood Indigo," "Never No Lament" (which, with lyrics, became "Do Nothing 'Til You Hear from Me"), and "It Don't Mean a Thing (If It Ain't Got That Swing)." Writing lyrics gives direct meaning to music and tells a story. Not all song lyrics have to rhyme, but rhyming and repetition help give a song its forward motion. Think like a lyricist, and try your hand at writing lyrics for a Duke Ellington song.

YOU'LL NEED

♪ CD player, computer, iPod, or other music listening device

♪ Recordings of "Mood Indigo," "Never No Lament," and "Do Nothing 'Til You Hear from Me"

♪ Pencil

♪ Paper

Listen to the musical selections listed, both with and without a singer. Then take your time listening to one of the collections off *Duke Ellington's Greatest Hits*; you will find that most of the tunes are instrumental numbers. Pick out one that has no words; it can be either a slow ballad or a swing-dance type tune. Figure out what kind of song form the tune has. Is it a 12-bar blues? Is it an AABA form, with 4-bar phrases? Think about the mood of the music, and let the sounds of the different soloists help you think about the lyrics. Performers like Johnny Hodges were so melodic you almost could believe you were hearing a human voice!

hall in America. On the night of the concert, Carnegie Hall was packed. In the jazz world, nothing of this magnitude had been presented in a concert hall since the 1924 premiere of *Rhapsody in Blue* by George Gershwin. That piece was Gershwin's introduction to the world as a serious composer.

"That first night at Carnegie was the only time in my life that I didn't have stage fright. I just didn't have time—I couldn't afford the luxury of being scared."

At intermission, Ellington was presented with a plaque signed by 32 noted musicians and composers from the classical and jazz worlds, including Aaron Copland, Leopold Stokowski, Marian Anderson, Paul Robeson, Count Basie, and Benny Goodman. Some of the reviews of this piece were harsh, especially from jazz critics who could not grasp what Ellington was striving toward. It wasn't until many years later that *Black, Brown and Beige* was recognized as the piece it truly was: "the elevation of jazz to an orchestral art."

All in all, the 1940s were productive years for Duke and his band. The band was again based in New York City, where they had landed a long-term residency at a nightclub for the first time in years. This was at the Hurricane, at 51st and Broadway in the heart of midtown Manhattan. Duke and the band were happy to be back, as New York City was home to several of its members. The Hurricane was a fancy nightclub with a huge floor for dancers and floor shows. Duke started his sets dramatically: a platform stage was lowered from the ceiling, with Duke seated at a piano draped in satin.

Finally, peace was at hand. In May 1945, Germany surrendered, followed by Japan in August. All over the world, people celebrated these victories, literally dancing in the streets. But the years following World War II turned out to be the end of the big dance band era, and the future of big bands looked bleak. In 1946, Duke's band suffered two losses in quick succession. Trombonist Tricky Sam Nanton, who had started with Duke at the Kentucky Club, died suddenly while the band was on tour. A few months later, alto saxophonist Otto Hardwick, one of the original Duke's Serenaders, left the band and music for good. Duke

Some Members of the Orchestra

LAWRENCE BROWN
Sweet or hot, his trombone is tops.

JOHNNY HODGES
On alto sax he is easily the king, year after year.

FREDDY GUY
He started with the Duke back in the old banjo days.

KAY DAVIS
Her vocal obbligatos are a highlight of Ellington's music.

JOYA SHERRILL
She's the girl who sings as pretty as she looks.

HARRY CARNEY
Baritone saxophonist. He's been the winner on his instrument in every poll.

Some members of the Duke Ellington Orchestra in the mid-1940s. Institute of Jazz Studies

and other big band leaders shared similar struggles: there was a lot of turnover among musicians, big projects were turned down, and dance halls and clubs felt that hiring 15- and 17-piece bands was too expensive. While most people eagerly anticipated new opportunities after the war, for the first time in many years Duke and his band faced an uncertain future. ∾

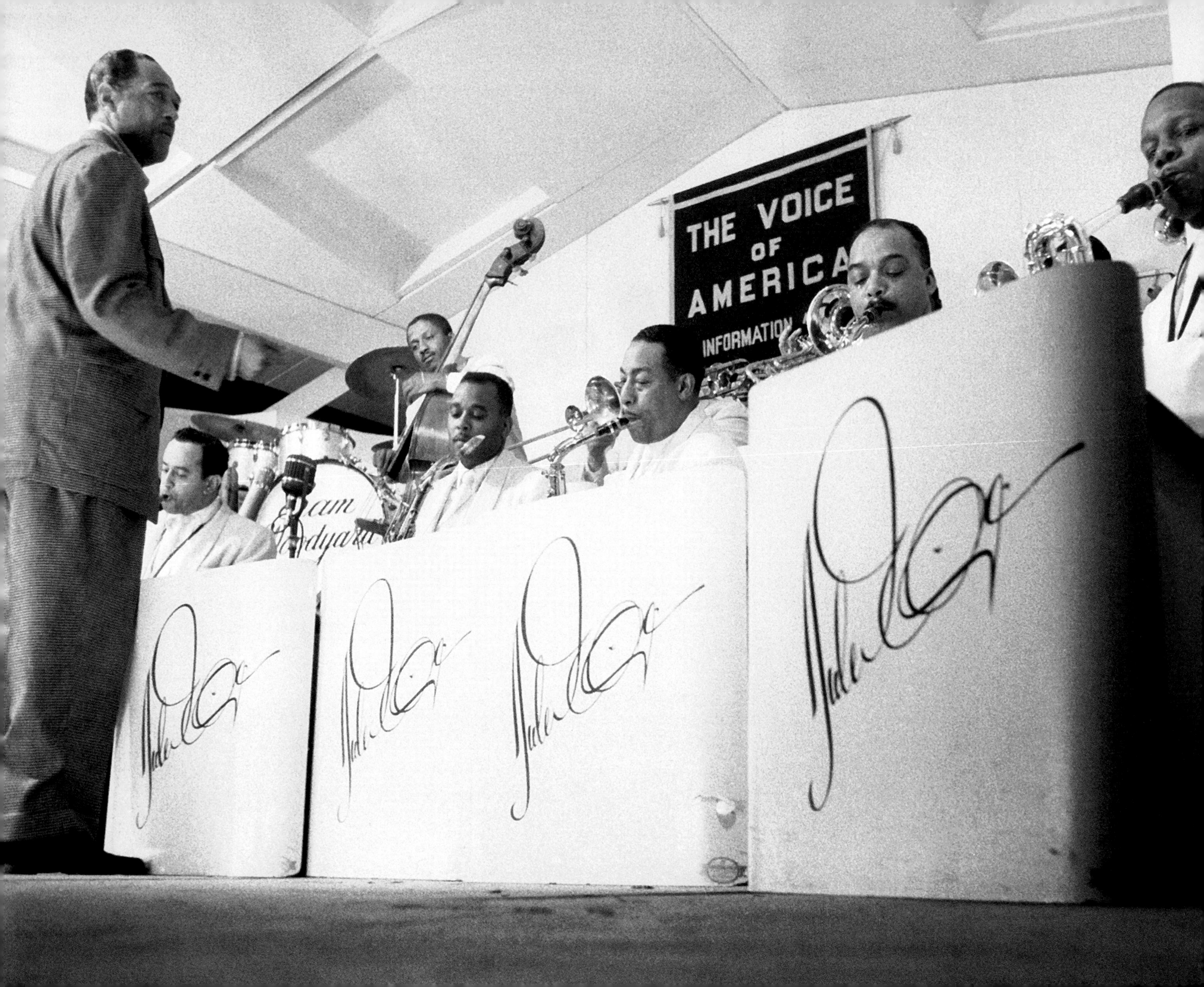
THE VOICE
OF
AMERICA
INFORMATION

8

THE COMEBACK KID

*I*n the years following Word War II, Duke and other top big band leaders struggled to get enough work to keep their bands together. This was much harder than 10 years earlier, when Duke had commanded top fees and the band played at the same place for weeks at a time. By the end of the 1940s, almost every major big band leader—Benny Goodman and Tommy Dorsey among them—made the hard decision to break up their big bands. In fact, one of the *only* big bands that stayed together was Duke's. The royalties Duke earned from his top songs supported the band through these lean times, even if it wasn't in the style of previous years. Now they often played one-nighters with long stretches of highway between jobs.

There were several changes during the postwar years that made the great big bands of the 1930s and 1940s seem like dinosaurs. Previously, Duke had been the pioneer, the experimenter—now different trends were taking over, socially and musically. Soldiers and sailors came home from World War II wanting to start families; instead of going out dancing,

An interesting photograph of the famous composer-arranger-leader Duke Ellington playing a Spinet or small piano which he favors.

Here Duke is explaining to the famous author Roi Ottley the different shadings and meanings of his successful concert work, "New World A'Comin'," based on Ottley's book.

Duke Ellington and his right-hand man and arranger, Billy "Swee'-pea" Strayhorn. His style of arranging and composing can hardly be distinguished from Ellington's.

Duke Ellington is the sponsor of a fund to send worthy musical students to famed Juilliard School of Music on free three-year scholarships. Recent winners: (l. to r.) Paul Rudoff and Elaine Jones, New York City and Warren Norwood, Forest Hills, N. Y.

Duke in the press, mid-1940s. Institute of Jazz Studies

Duke **ELLINGTON**

and his Famous **ORCHESTRA**

METROPOLITAN OPERA HOUSE CONCERT PROGRAM

SUNDAY EVENING, JANUARY 21, 1951

Program for a concert at the Metropolitan Opera, New York, 1951. Courtesy Morris Hodara

they stayed home on weekends. Popular singers like Frank Sinatra had become big stars during the war and displaced the big band leaders' importance in the record business. The "new thing" in jazz was a small-band instrumental style called bebop, and younger players such as trumpeter Dizzy Gillespie and saxophonist Charlie Parker were attracting a lot of attention. Small clubs, not huge ballrooms, became the places to hear jazz. Also, a new style called rock 'n' roll was just beginning to catch on with teenagers. Soon the biggest change of all in entertainment would show up in American living rooms—a box called a television.

Through all the changes, Ellington went his own way just as he always had. He needed to keep the band working so that his musicians could make a living. As a composer, he needed them to play his music. Over several decades, Duke's orchestra was the voice for the compositions he could not stop creating.

Though the big band era was waning, the name Duke Ellington still meant a lot to people in the entertainment world. In June 1949, Duke and the band appeared for the first time on television. The show was a special called *Adventures in Jazz*. But television performances were not yet as professional as they are today. Some critics pointed out that the show was sloppy, and one reviewer even noticed that one of the musicians fell asleep on stage.

HOME ENTERTAINMENT—TELEVISION

In 1920, Philo Taylor Farnsworth, a 14-year-old boy with a love of electronics, visualized how radio waves could be recomposed, line by line, to produce visual images. This idea came to him while he was mowing rows of hay on his father's farm in Idaho. When Farnsworth was 20, he devised a television set, for which he secured a patent. Though this was one of the great inventions of the 20th century, several factors delayed the availability of television sets for consumers, as well as recognition of young Farnsworth's contribution. Affordable television sets finally became available in the 1940s, and their popularity rose dramatically. In 1945 there were about 7,000 working television sets in American homes; by 1953, there were 20 million. Today, there are probably over 219 million TVs in the United States, and many families own two or more.

Television was a breakthrough in the media world, and in the world of entertainment: suddenly a band like Duke's could be seen by millions of people—far more than the biggest ballroom could ever hold.

At this point, Duke was 50 years old, and he and his men were thought of as old-timers. Keeping up a high level of performance under the grueling traveling conditions of the war and postwar years was hard on everyone, even Duke. Duke, Hodges, Greer, and Carney had been together now for 18 years touring. Imagine being with a large family that was almost always traveling! Morale was low. Duke even stopped writing new compositions for a while. When performing, the band relied on their old

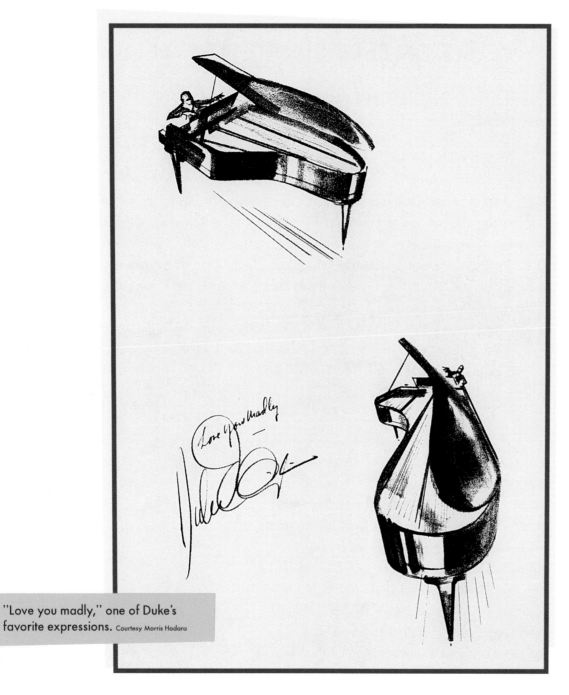

hits, like "Mood Indigo," "Sophisticated Lady," and "Take the 'A' Train." When Duke's friendliest rival, Count Basie, finally broke up his big band in 1950, rumors were flying that the end was in sight for Duke Ellington and His Orchestra, too.

To reinspire himself and his band, Duke booked a tour to Europe in the spring of 1950. They were still received like royalty, and tremendous crowds flocked to welcome them everywhere they traveled. They played 74 concerts in 77 days in France, Belgium, Holland, and Scandinavia.

Their trip was such a success that Duke was ready to compose again. When he returned home, he finished a big, new composition called *Harlem*, which was a huge hit at its premiere at an NAACP concert in early 1951. But, just a few weeks later, disaster struck the heart of the band.

In one swoop, Johnny Hodges, Sonny Greer, and Lawrence Brown announced they were leaving Duke's band to work in a band led by Hodges! These three musicians, all of whom had been with Duke for decades, had plotted the details in secret. The new band would be known as Johnny Hodges and His Orchestra.

This was the most wounding betrayal Duke had ever experienced from his musicians. Why and how could this ever happen? Duke had been a bandleader for almost 30 years; he had seen several of his best, most loyal musicians come and go—often with his blessing. But Hodges and the velvety sound of his saxophone were at the very core of the Ellington Orchestra's sound. Duke couldn't believe he had been so deceived.

Hodges had been hatching this plan for at least two years. In addition to his work with Duke, Johnny Hodges was one of the stars of a new series of concerts called *Jazz at the Philharmonic*, organized by a manager named Norman Granz. Granz urged Johnny to start his own group as a way to become famous on his own and to make more money. Hodges, though one of Ellington's top-paid musicians, always grumbled about what Duke paid him. Hodges also saw the world of big bands crumbling around him. To make matters worse, Johnny went public with his complaints about Duke's compositions: "We didn't like the new stuff and the tone poems so much." This betrayal sent rumors flying about Duke disbanding, or moving to Hollywood to write music for movies and television.

But to all the critics and gossipers, Ellington firmly responded: "Absolutely ridiculous." Duke worked quickly to replace his musicians, and pulled off what became known as "the Great James Robbery." He managed to recruit his former trombone player and composer Juan Tizol, who had been working with

Ellington and Johnny Hodges at a recording session, 1957. Photo by Don Hunstein; courtesy Don Hunstein and SONY/BMG Archives

Harry James's new big band. Two other musicians in James's band also joined up: drummer Louis Bellson and saxophonist Willie Smith. They both adored Ellington's music and were first-rate musicians. For them, the chance to play with Duke was irresistible, even if the big band era was over. Critics and Ellington fans flipped over Louis Bellson, a great drummer and the first white musician to join the Ellington Orchestra.

The game of musical chairs continued through the 1950s. Duke hired several younger musicians, such as saxophonist Paul Gonsalves and trumpeter Clark Terry. The new members reenergized Duke and everyone else. Duke started writing pieces expressly for his new musicians, just as he had in previous years.

Sheet music cover for "Satin Doll."
Institute of Jazz Studies

This new band was soon as celebrated for its sound and style as any in Duke's past. But right now, times continued to be tough. The fancy movie theaters of the past were closed, or didn't hire big bands for stage shows anymore. Duke's audience was aging along with him. Duke struggled to support his family and his band and staff—who, to Duke, were family, too.

Still, Duke was a star who wouldn't fade, and he continued to be a media pioneer. While performing in Los Angeles in 1951, Duke and the band were invited to make soundies for television. The band videotaped four tunes, called "telescriptions," which were shown on various TV stations for years. Duke and the band also appeared in "TV specials" early on, and Duke was on several celebrity quiz shows. Duke thought that television could rescue the world of the big bands, and he participated in as many broadcasts as he could.

Unfortunately, in this case, Duke's media instincts did not prove correct. Though there were many TV shows or specials that involved jazz in the 1950s and 1960s, television did not prove to rescue the world of big jazz bands. During the 1950s, popular singers were getting the most attention on TV, and soon shows featured the sounds of rock 'n' roll.

Another new format held more promise: the long-playing (LP) record, which held

Activity
Make a Phonograph Needle

TODAY MOST PEOPLE listen to music on CDs, or download music to iPod-like devices or to their computers. But people from an older generation (maybe your parents, and most likely your grandparents and older relatives) used old-fashioned phonographs or record players to play records. In the 1950s, record players had adapters for playing the three disk formats that were available: 78 rpms, 45 rpms, and 33⅓ rpms. The records were made out of vinyl disks. The grooves of the records (which contained the recorded music as electronic information) were originally etched onto wax disks called masters; the masters were then pressed as vinyl disk copies. These disks were then played back on a turntable, with a sensitive needle (the best ones were made with low-grade diamonds). The needle would vibrate in response to the grooves; the vibrations would get transferred as sound waves through an amplifier, reproducing the recorded music. Try this project yourself, so you can discover how a needle can make music.

YOU'LL NEED
- ♪ Turntable and record album (your older relatives might have these items, or you can find them at a thrift store or garage sale)
- ♪ Long straight pin
- ♪ Plastic drinking cup, approximately 4 inches high
- ♪ Clay or play dough
- ♪ Magnifying glass

First, explore the grooves in the record with a magnifying glass. You will see that the grooves on the record are full of tiny bumps and valleys; these grooves are a copy of the master recording's etched grooves. Push the pin, which will be your phonograph nee-

dle, through the bottom of the plastic cup from the inside. Then press a small ball of the clay or play dough on the head of the pin (inside the cup) to hold the pin steady. Place a record on the turntable and turn the power on. Gently swing the turntable's horizontal balance arm, which holds the real phonograph needle, out of the way. While keeping your hand steady, hold the cup gently above the record so that the straight pin slightly drags along a groove as the record goes around.

Do you hear any music? The vibration of the needle produces sound as it goes over the grooves, and the sound is then amplified by the cup. Was the sound at all clear? What happens if you apply more pressure on the needle? What happens to the sound when you change the turntable's speed? What are other factors that might affect the clarity of the sound?

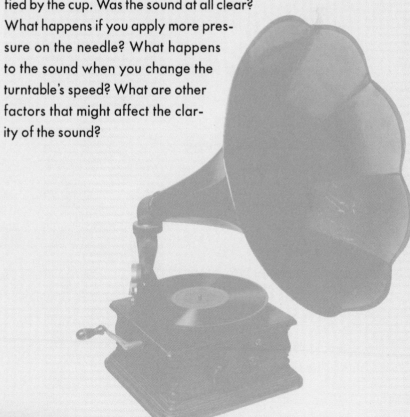

Design an Album Jacket

IN THE 1950s, record album cover design became an art form in itself. Record companies realized that appealing cover designs attracted people's attention; album cover design became as huge a sales tool as sheet music covers had been early in the 20th century. There were several artists and designers who enjoyed specializing in this format, and used a variety of mediums to create covers: watercolor, oil paint, pastel, pen and ink, and collage.

These two Ellington album covers show different approaches. The design for *The Mooche*, with its stylized piano and hands, is witty and kind of abstract. The cover for *Liberian Suite* (which Duke was commissioned to compose to celebrate Liberia's centennial) is more like an illustration, with colorful ships bringing settlers to the newly formed republic. Try your hand at designing an album cover for your favorite band or musical composition.

with your design. How can your design tell the viewer about the music? What colors best express the music?

Before you start making sketches, write down all the information that will appear on the album cover: the title, the name of the musician or band, and the titles of the most important songs or compositions (you don't need to list every single one). The type will be part of your design. Once you start sketching your ideas, block out where the type elements ought to go. Once you have settled on the design, measure out a 12 × 12-inch square on large sketchbook paper for your final version. Pencil in the design. Then, whether you use a printout for the type or do your own calligraphy, allow room for the words. Color in your final version with watercolors, markers, or whatever color medium you prefer. Then either glue on the type or do your own lettering for the final step.

YOU'LL NEED

♪ Recording of a favorite song
♪ CD, cassette player, iPod, or other music listening device
♪ Pencil
♪ Scrap paper
♪ Scissors
♪ 12 × 12-inch sketchbook paper
♪ Computer for type fonts (optional)
♪ Colored markers, crayons, watercolors

Pick out a favorite CD or musical composition that you would like to create an album cover for. Listen to the music several times while you think about what image you want to convey

30 minutes of music on each side. The LP was first introduced to the public in 1950. Other advances in recording technology, such as high-fidelity (hi-fi) and stereophonic (stereo) sound reproduction, soon followed. Hi-fi, stereo, and cleaner recording techniques set off the beauty of Duke's music more than ever before on record, so much so that *Ellington Uptown in Hi-Fi* became a favorite demo record for hi-fi salespeople during the mid-1950s.

The longer records were perfect for the more expansive pieces Ellington wanted to write and record. But while these pieces appealed to the sophisticated listeners who were now Duke's core audience, he still wanted to make a hit record—like he did in the old days, not just one, but hit after hit after hit.

Even with their occasional successes, the band struggled for recognition and jobs between 1951 and 1956. There were no more movie invitations, no overseas tours, and no steady radio broadcasts—just lots of one-nighters. Duke even took a job for six weeks as accompanist for a water show with ice skaters called the Aquacade in Queens, at the site of the future home of the 1964 World's Fair. He played a medley of hits on the piano, and then another conductor led a different band with strings. This steady job helped keep the band together for those few weeks. More than anything, Ellington wanted and needed his band.

"I like to keep a band so I can write and hear the music the next day," Duke often said. Just as important, Duke really loved being in front of the bandstand playing to a live audience. This was what he lived for; the band was his life. "We're not one of those people who stay in business only so long as business is good. We stay in it 52 weeks a year. . . . The fun of writing and participating in music is the motivating force that keeps us going on and on." Through these years, Duke tried to put a positive spin on things. He did not like to be seen as failing or having a hard time, no matter what.

Finally, in late summer of 1955, Duke's fortune changed for the better again. Trombonist Lawrence Brown left Johnny Hodges's band and returned to Duke—which caused Hodges's band to break up. Soon, Johnny Hodges rejoined Duke too—though no one really knows who approached whom to make up. In truth, Johnny Hodges had a hard time being a bandleader. The job involved many responsibilities to make sure things ran smoothly. Johnny was not so good at delegating, or at thinking of all the details. He was happy to be back as Duke's foremost soloist, and Duke was happy to have him. The saxophone section was complete once again.

Around the same time, a new drummer named Sam Woodyard replaced Louis Bellson, who was leaving. Sam proved to be another perfect drummer for the band at this time; modern but swinging, forceful but always musical. Sam saw the band through its late period. Now there were several new personalities—younger musicians like Clark Terry, Paul Gonsalves, trombonist Britt Woodman, and bassist Jimmy Woode—alongside the old guard, Harry Carney, Juan Tizol, and Johnny Hodges. Mercer, who had worked on and off for his father, returned as an assistant manager and copyist. It was a great combination of old and new voices.

But what really brought the band back to life was the return of Ellington's magic touch for being in the right place at the right time. The band was invited to appear at the Newport Jazz Festival in July 1956. Only in its third year, the Newport Jazz Festival in Rhode Island had al-

Duke Ellington and His Orchestra at the Newport Jazz Festival, July 1956. Photo by Don Hunstein; courtesy Don Hunstein and SONY/BMG Archives

ready become a popular destination, complete with live jazz against a backdrop of sea, sand, and stars.

Duke was scheduled to perform at midnight on the second night of concerts. He was a little upset because the crowd had already thinned out by then. The band performed *Newport Festival Suite,* which Duke had written for the occasion, but which now didn't seem that exciting. So Duke chose an older blues tune to play next: "Diminuendo and Crescendo in Blue." It was late at night, and the danceable beat struck a chord in the musicians and audience alike. When the tenor saxophonist Paul Gonsalves got up to take his solo, Duke started egging him on. Gonsalves stood at the edge of the stage and played chorus after chorus, building in intensity, the band shouting along with him. Suddenly, a beautiful woman got up and started dancing, and the crowd went wild. Couples started dancing and people rushed to the edge of the stage. The band finally left the stage, after several encores, at 1:00 A.M., with everyone cheering for more.

The word was out. Duke Ellington and his band were back—the hit comeback, the sensation of the festival. The next day, everyone was talking about Paul's 27 blues choruses—and the crowd's crazy response. People felt they had been to one of the most exciting concerts ever. Almost immediately, Duke and his band were headliners again. Ellington at Newport was the turning point that brought Duke's band back into the public eye. Years later, Duke still remarked with joy: "I was born in 1956 at the Newport Jazz Festival." ∞

9

DUKE ON TOUR– AROUND THE WORLD IN 80 DAYS

*T*hat single night at the Newport Jazz Festival, July 7, 1956, revived the fortunes of Duke and his band. Once again, the band was rolling. A few weeks later, "Jazzman Duke Ellington" made the cover of *Time* magazine, with a far better story than the magazine had first planned on, thanks to Newport. From then on, Duke Ellington, his band, and music were never again considered has-beens or outdated. Duke's success at Newport catapulted him into a high plateau of fame for the rest of his life.

Engineers from Columbia Records had recorded almost everything that went on at the Newport festival, and caught the band's incredible comeback set. The next day, a Columbia producer approached Duke with the best recording contract he'd had for a long time: Duke would alternate recording albums of new compositions with LPs filled with his popular hits. This was just the kind of contract Duke needed and wanted. That September, Columbia released *Ellington at Newport*, which was an immediate hit album and one of Duke's bestselling albums ever.

Right away, Duke and Strayhorn started working on new pieces to record, especially jazz suites and long works. As collaborators they were never at a loss for ideas. Duke relied on Strayhorn to keep working while Duke was on the road with the band. Between 1956 and 1962, Duke's band recorded 20 LPs' worth of material for Columbia, and also recorded 150 other projects. Duke was once again on the go all the time: on tour, appearing on TV, composing for movies and other special projects. The new pieces he and Strayhorn created were rehearsed and even performed in concerts while the band was on tour; their favorites were recorded when the band returned to New York.

Duke's renewed visibility was infectious. Suddenly other bandleaders of the swing era, Count Basie among them, began enjoying new interest and pulled their big bands back together. Like Duke's band, these new big bands were a mix of elder jazz statesman and younger musicians who had a more modern sound, influenced by bebop. The big band dances that were the lifeblood of the 1930s and 1940s gave

Duke Ellington and Billy Strayhorn at a recording session, 1957. Photo by Don Hunstein; courtesy Don Hunstein and SONY/BMG Archives

way to concerts, jazz festivals, TV appearances, and college tours. These veteran bandleaders discovered that they and their bands were not museum pieces; the new musicians gave their music an edge, yet their bands still had a powerful swing and unity.

During these years, Duke created one masterwork after another. The first was called *A Drum Is a Woman*. He and Billy Strayhorn composed this suite for a new album, but it quickly became a bigger project. *A Drum Is a Woman* was dramatized for the first TV jazz spectacular; it was also the first live TV broadcast of a show by an all-black cast. "Music history and television history were made on the night of the 8th of May," wrote one reviewer, "The show was a sumptuous wedding of visual and aural delights." A myth of the origin of jazz, *A Drum Is a Woman* is about a character named Madame Zzaj (jazz spelled backward) who traces the history of jazz from its African roots to the Caribbean, to swing and on to bebop—then finally to the moon. Duke considered this composition one of his finest achievements.

In the fall of 1956, Duke's band played at the Shakespeare Festival in Ontario, Canada,

Duke and Count Basie collaborate for the album *First Time: The Duke Meets the Count*, 1961.

Photo by Don Hunstein; courtesy Don Hunstein and SONY/BMG Archives

Activity
Write Liner Notes for a CD

DURING THE 1950s and 1960s, one of the most informative sources about jazz was "liner notes." These were essays on the back covers of record albums that included information about the musicians themselves, and special notes about the compositions or the recording session. In the 1980s, when compact discs became the new format for recorded music, jazz liner notes were then printed in the CD booklets, carrying on the same tradition. Many noted music journalists have contributed to the literature about jazz in this way. Think like a music journalist, and write a set of liner notes.

YOU'LL NEED
♪ Choice of favorite CDs
♪ Computer and printer (optional)
♪ Pencil
♪ Paper

Read the excerpt to the right from the liner notes for a CD of *Jelly Roll Morton's Greatest Hits*. Then pick out one of your favorite CDs that you would like to write about. It can be any style of music you like: rock, rap, a Broadway show, folk music, jazz, or a classical symphony. Write down the album's title and the musicians involved. You can use this example as a model, but there are no hard and fast rules for writing liner notes. Mainly, you want to include information about the recording and the performance that will enhance people's experience of listening to the music. So if it was a "live" recording, it's nice to include details about the event (especially if you were there!). It's also good to include a brief biography of the musicians or a history of the band. Then you can briefly discuss your favorite songs on the CD, and what makes this particular recording special. In the process, you'll enjoy listening to the music all over again!

Jelly Roll Morton claimed to be the inventor of Jazz. By the time he was 12, in 1902, he was already playing ragtime piano and dance music in Storyville, the famed district of his native New Orleans. A pioneering pianist, whose inventive left hand helped ragtime piano head toward the "stride" style, he was one of the first important jazz composers and arrangers. He achieved his greatest fame between 1926 and 1930, when he made a series of hit records in Chicago with his recording group, the Red Hot Peppers. His skilled arrangements of tunes here like "Black Bottom Stomp" and "Doctor Jazz" combined short sizzling solos with carefully worked out New Orleans-style passages.

which presented jazz concerts alongside classic drama. For this occasion, Duke and Strayhorn composed a suite called *Such Sweet Thunder*. The different sections were musical portraits of favorite Shakespearian characters, such as Puck, Romeo and Juliet, Hamlet, and Lady Macbeth, translated through the unique voices of Duke's musicians. One of Duke's most charming works, *Such Sweet Thunder* was later presented in New York City at a "Music for Moderns" concert, and led to a commission by the Ontario festival for Duke to write background music for Shakespeare's *Timon of Athens*.

Coincidentally, the Ellington Orchestra as a whole was finally allowed to perform in Great Britain in 1958. American big bands had been banned from touring Great Britain since the late 1930s because of the strict rules of the British musicians' union, which did not want its members deprived of work. Duke's band was the first allowed to tour England, in exchange for a British big band's tour of the United States.

The band arrived in London to a thunderous welcome in October 1958, and one of the highlights was performing for members of the royal family. That evening, Queen Elizabeth formally received Duke and seven other guests. This was one of Duke Ellington's most treasured moments in a life filled with many:

"I was so impressed by Her Majesty because I noticed that she spoke differently to every person who was presented to her. She spoke French to the French, German to the Germans, and when she spoke to me, she spoke American-English. She was very casual and we talked a lot. She told me about all the records of mine her father [King George] had."

When Duke returned to the United States, he started concentrating on a new suite dedicated to Queen Elizabeth. He recorded *The Queen's Suite* in February 1959. He only allowed one copy of the record to be made at that time, and it was sent to the Queen. This special recording was finally made available to the public after Duke died in 1974, according to his wishes. Duke had other ways of commemorating his moments with the Queen, too. According to trumpeter Rex Stewart, for months afterward, Duke—a real clotheshorse—did not change shoes between sets like he usually did; he wore the same dress shoes he wore at his meeting with Queen Elizabeth.

On April 29, 1959, Duke Ellington turned 60 years old. Over the next decade, his pace, if anything, speeded up. For the first time in 25 years he was asked to write music for a film.

Queen Elizabeth II and Duke Ellington in London, 1958.
Institute of Jazz Studies

His soundtrack album for the movie *Anatomy of a Murder* ended up winning a Grammy. Meanwhile, commissions for other film scores, TV themes (including the *Asphalt Jungle*), and other projects came streaming in. He also started receiving awards and honors regularly. One that he truly treasured was the NAACP's Spingarn Medal, given to him for the "Highest or noblest achievement by an American Negro during the preceding year or years."

Recording session for the movie *Anatomy of a Murder,* 1959. Photo by Don Hunstein; courtesy Don Hunstein and SONY/BMG Archives

DUKE IN THE 1960s

Ellington's band—as always—was his pride and joy. But as his musicians aged along with him, there was a lot of turnover in the band, including some returnees. Trumpet player Cootie Williams returned in 1962 after an absence of 22 years; trombonist Lawrence Brown also returned after a lengthy break. For many jazz musicians—young and old— Duke's music was still the best around, and the pay was better than most, or more than some of his aging musicians, no matter how legendary, could earn on their own. So, amazingly, in the 1960s, Duke had four musicians who had first played with him decades earlier: Harry Carney, Johnny Hodges, Cootie Williams, and Lawrence Brown. There were others who had worked with him almost as long. His writing partner Billy Strayhorn had now been with him for almost 20 years. Many other musicians had spent the peak years of their careers with Duke: Ray Nance, Jimmy Hamilton, Paul Gonsalves, Clark Terry, and Russell Procope.

Additionally, by the 1960s, the Ellington songbook was a rich treasure-trove; songs such as "Mood Indigo," "Satin Doll," "Do Nothing 'Til You Hear from Me," "Sophisticated Lady," and many more were on a par with those by other masters of Tin Pan Alley, such as George and Ira Gershwin, Richard Rodgers and Lorenz Hart, and Jerome Kern. They were recorded by the best pop singers of that time, such as Ella Fitzgerald and Frank Sinatra, and even by the new wave of jazz musicians like saxophonist John Coltrane and bassist Charles Mingus.

The 1960s were also a time of upheaval. It was a landmark decade for civil rights; incidents both violent and peaceful paved the way for the monumental March on Washington of 1963, led by Dr. Martin Luther King Jr., and the Civil Rights Act of 1964. As ever, Duke made his beliefs known not so much through public appearances or statements, but through his music. In this, he was following through on decades of compositions, going back to *Creole Rhapsody* (1928), and *Black, Brown and Beige* (1943). Many of his compositions were a celebration of African American life. In September 1963, he created another such work with *My People*, a revue commissioned for a big exposition in Chicago, the Century of Negro Progress Exposition, a month-long multimedia event. *My People* was a huge production that included Duke's band, a choir, the Alvin Ailey dancers, and several actors. Duke threw himself into the production, and even helped build and paint the sets. *My People* had roots in Ellington's former large works, and included songs that bordered on gospel and the

Activity
Host a Jam Session

DUKE AND HIS musicians often took part in jam sessions, which are part of a long tradition in jazz. Jam sessions are informal get-togethers for musicians; they can take place at people's homes, in parks, or in jazz clubs, after regular shows are over. They give musicians the opportunity to play without the pressure of a big audience, to hear talented young musicians they might not have heard before, and to play music with people they normally don't perform with. Decades ago, legendary "cutting contests" (competitions) took place at jam sessions among the greatest names in jazz, such as saxophonists Ben Webster, who played with Duke Ellington in the 1940s, and Lester Young, who played with Count Basie. Musicians would try to outdo each other with their improvisational skills. Gather up some friends and host a jam session.

YOU'LL NEED

♪ Several friends
♪ Jug tubas, kazoos, washtub bass, autoharp, drum sticks, coffee cans, and other instruments you've built or used while reading this book
♪ Piano, electric keyboard, guitar, drums, or other musical instruments

♪ Recordings of familiar Ellington tunes, such as "C-Jam Blues," "Mood Indigo," "Take the 'A' Train," and "Satin Doll"
♪ CD player, computer, iPod, or other music listening device
♪ Beverages of your choice
♪ Party corn bread and other snacks

Ask your parents if you can host a jam session for your friends. Hold the session where it's OK to make a lot of noise. Before the date, gather up the instruments you have made or that you own; see what your friends can bring. When everyone is together, try to decide on two or three tunes to work on. For instance, "C-Jam Blues" is a tune that is easy to learn. Play it a few times on your CD player. Then try to play it together on your chosen instruments, and pick two or three people among yourselves who want to try to improvise. Then choose another tune, like "Take the 'A' Train," and do the same thing. Throughout your session, make sure that whoever wants to improvise eventually gets a turn, even if it's only for a few measures. Have a good time jammin'!

blues, slow ballads, and jumping dance numbers. While Duke was in Chicago, he finally had the opportunity to meet Martin Luther King Jr., to whom he dedicated the show. One of the numbers was "King Fit the Battle of Alabam"—about the violent encounters Dr. King and his marchers endured with the state police in Birmingham, Alabama.

During 1963 and 1964, Duke's band traveled more widely than ever. In January 1963, they returned to Europe for a two-month tour that took them to London, Paris, Stockholm, and other major cities. As in previous trips, they were greeted by happy crowds, and their concerts sold out everywhere. But the constant travel was exhausting; most of Duke's men

ELLA FITZGERALD

Ella Fitzgerald (1917–1996), the "first lady of song" and the "first lady of scat," was the most popular American female jazz singer for over 50 years. Her story, like that of many other legendary jazz artists, was full of surprises and well-deserved opportunities. At the age of 17, Fitzgerald got the chance to compete at the Apollo Theater's Amateur Night—the *American Idol* contest of its time. At the last minute, she backed out of doing her dance routine and sang instead, winning the prize and setting in motion an amazing career. Soon she was singing with Chick Webb's Orchestra at Harlem's Savoy Ballroom, the prime showcase of swing and jazz in the 1930s. When Webb, her mentor as well as bandleader, died in 1938, Fitzgerald, who just a few years earlier had performed for pennies on the street, became the band's new leader. That same year, her scat version of the nursery rhyme "A-Tisket, A-Tasket" sold one million copies and made Ella Fitzgerald a household name.

Years later, Fitzgerald recorded a treasury of American songwriters with her songbook series. *Ella Fitzgerald Sings the Duke Ellington Songbook* was the only album on which she sang with the composer and his band. Duke and Billy Strayhorn wrote two new pieces just for her: "The E and D Blues" and "A Portrait of Ella Fitzgerald."

were in their 50s and 60s and not as energetic as they had been decades earlier. Said trumpeter Cootie Williams: "Up early, run to the airport, and get on the plane. Sitting around the airport all day, you get into a different country to sit at the airport only to go play the concert, and you play two concerts and get to bed around twelve, one o'clock and you're up at six the next morning." Their music and the constant admiration from their audiences pulled them through, again and again.

"We used to travel mostly by trains —big old romantic hooting trains. Then it was all buses and automobiles, with occasional leisurely comfortable ships as the foreign picture opened up. Today jets have expanded our field of action out of all recognition."

In 1963, Duke and his band were asked to do their first tour for the U.S. State Department. Starting in the mid-1950s, several prominent

A greeting for Duke Ellington on his first State Department tour to the Mideast and Far East, 1963.
Institute of Jazz Studiesv

THE JAZZ AMBASSADORS

In the mid-1950s, at the height of the Cold War with what was then the Soviet Union, the U.S. State Department decided to send a new kind of ambassador abroad to help promote democracy and foster good relations with developing countries. In 1956, the great jazz trumpeter Dizzy Gillespie was asked to lead the first jazz State Department tour, and he took an integrated big band to the Middle East. From then through the 1970s, some of the finest American jazz musicians traveled to the far corners of the globe on similar missions.

Ellington's first State Department tour took the band to major cities in Jordan, Syria, Afghanistan, India, and Pakistan. They performed at least two scheduled concerts in each city; at times to monumental crowds (the opening concert in Damascus, Syria, drew 17,000 people). Other State Department tours took Duke's band to the Soviet Union, all through South America and Latin America, and to the Far East. At every stop, Duke and his musicians had daily receptions, luncheons, and dinners with ambassadors, diplomats, and VIPs. Years later, clarinetist Jimmy Hamilton said that the band performed too much for dignitaries and not enough for regular people.

Why did the U.S. government choose jazz, among all the musical forms, to promote abroad? Because as an art form, jazz was born and bred in America, and as an African American art form, jazz was considered an expression of democratic ideals and racial equality. Jazz was an important cultural export in the years when the civil rights struggle and the Vietnam War were damaging America's image abroad. Louis Armstrong, Duke Ellington, Dizzy Gillespie, and many other musicians wore the public face of African American pride and accomplishment. Yet some of the musicians—backstage and onstage—were more outspoken about race and politics than the State Department had anticipated.

The musicians' candor and generosity toward worldwide audiences and their openness to new experiences made the "jazz ambassadors" program a success, and added to the recognition of jazz as a universal music.

Duke Ellington and His Orchestra at a dance performance in Ceylon, 1963. Institute of Jazz Studies

jazz musicians, including Dizzy Gillespie and Louis Armstrong, had embarked on such tours. Jazz was a common denominator the world over, even though in America, jazz music no longer had the universal appeal of the big band years. Abroad, though, concerts by "jazz ambassadors" eased the way for diplomatic relations in many foreign countries. Interestingly, because Ellington had performed so many benefit concerts for war relief and civil rights, the FBI had opened a file on him and suspected him of having Communist ties during the Cold War era. By this time, State Department officials felt that Duke was a perfect choice for sponsored diplomacy. His tour of the Mideast in the fall of 1963 was an amazing journey through Jordan, Syria, India, and Pakistan. A few months later the band went to Japan for the first time.

Through the 1960s, Duke received many honors and acknowledgments. During President Lyndon Johnson's term from 1964 to 1968, Duke and the band performed at the White House several times, and Duke was presented with the President's Gold Medal. In 1969, a special tribute took place in honor of Duke Ellington's 70th birthday, and President Richard Nixon gave Duke the Presidential Medal of Freedom, the highest recognition the U.S. government could give him. Duke's mentor— from decades long past—Willie "The Lion"

"After thirteen different shots and vaccinations, we leave New York on September 6, 1963, for one of the most unusual and adventurous trips we have ever undertaken. We change planes in Rome and go on to Damascus, the first stop in a tour for the U.S. Department of State."

Duke and the band are greeted in Ceylon, 1963.
Institute of Jazz Studies

125

Smith, played a duet with Duke, and politicians, family members, and musicians were all present. This event was the honor of a lifetime. Duke Ellington, the grandchild of ex-slaves, whose own father had served as a caterer at White House functions, lived to see his dreams and that of his parents fulfilled: a life in the arts of his own making, with dignity, beauty, and justice for all who crossed his path.

Along with the glory came sad news. In early 1964, Billy Strayhorn was diagnosed with advanced cancer. At first, this didn't slow Strayhorn down, and Duke kept track of him, as did Dr. Logan, Duke's longtime personal doctor.

At the same time, Duke was given an opportunity for a project that turned into one of the most meaningful of his life. While touring the West Coast, he was asked to compose a concert—the *Sacred Concert*—for Grace Cathedral in San Francisco. This came as a complete surprise. The cathedral's leaders knew his music well; they were familiar with his gospel-like songs like "Come Sunday" and the show *My People*. Duke was not asked to

Reunited: Willie "The Lion" Smith, one of Duke's early piano mentors, and Duke at the All-Star White House Tribute, 1969.
Institute of Jazz Studies

create a jazz mass, following the true sections of a mass; he was asked to create the music he was known for, with the deep spiritual feeling some of his compositions clearly had. Immediately, Duke knew his *Sacred Concert* would start with "In the Beginning God," and he accepted this wonderful assignment.

Sadly, this gift of a project coincided with Billy Strayhorn's worsening illness. Duke said, "I was in California or Vegas or somewhere, and he was in the hospital in New York. I called him up because the doctor said keep his mind busy, don't let him sit around and think. So I told him what I was doing. Billy Strayhorn took those six syllables [In the Beginning God] and wrote a theme." Just as so many times before, Duke's and Billy's starting notes were the same. The project progressed quickly while the band was on tour in Nevada and California, and they started rehearsing sections as soon as Ellington and Strayhorn had the music ready. Meanwhile, the choral director and chorus in San Francisco started rehearsing their parts. The entire group of performers did not get to hear everything together until they were all in San Francisco.

The first *Concert of Sacred Music* was performed at Grace Cathedral on September 16, 1965, then again, the day after Christmas in New York City, at the Fifth Avenue Presbyterian Church. Three years later, a *Second Sacred Concert*, with additional pieces (and some revisions), would premiere at the Cathedral of St. John the Divine in New York City. A *Third Sacred Concert* would be performed in the grandest cathedral of all, Westminster Abbey in London, just seven months before Duke's death in 1974. These wondrous works, which

THE PROTESTANT COUNCIL
    OF THE CITY OF NEW YORK
AND

THE FIFTH AVENUE
    PRESBYTERIAN CHURCH

PRESENT

a concert of sacred music

BY

duke ellington

SUNDAY, DECEMBER 26, 1965
NEW YORK CITY
EIGHT O'CLOCK AND MIDNIGHT

Program for *A Concert of Sacred Music*, 1965. Courtesy Morris Hodara

included roles for vocalists, a choir, dancers, and a narrator, represent a large part of the last phase of his long career.

Over the next two years, Duke and the band toured almost nonstop. Mercer, who had taken other jobs for a few years, was back as general manager and section trumpet player. He would remain with the band through Duke's last years, and the two were very close.

During this same period, Billy Strayhorn's advanced cancer of the esophagus was spreading. He no longer traveled with the band, but kept composing and arranging for the band when he could, through several hospital stays.

An unusually tired Duke Ellington at a recording session.
Photo by Don Hunstein; courtesy of Don Hunstein and SONY/BMG Archives

In the last months of his life, Strayhorn revised a piece called "Blood Count" (blood tests were given frequently to cancer patients to monitor the disease) and sent it by messenger from his hospital bed to Carnegie Hall for a performance. Another piece Billy wrote during this time was titled "UMMG" (Upper Manhattan Medical Group). Duke's band played these two tunes often; they were swinging, joyful, and raucous, with melodies tinged with irony and passion.

Billy Strayhorn died on May 31, 1967; he was only 51 years old. His death was as devastating for Duke as that of his parents; the two collaborators had been very close, and Duke relied on Billy for so much. "Billy Strayhorn was my right arm, my left arm, all the eyes in the back of my head, my brainwaves in his head, and his in mine." Many admirers commented that it was hard to tell where Duke's writing ended and Billy's began. The other band members were also heartbroken. Three months after Strayhorn died, the band recorded an entire album of his compositions.

Billy Strayhorn. Courtesy David Hajdu

And His Mother Called Him Bill is a heartfelt tribute to a life devoted to music, beauty, and art, most of which was expressed by Duke Ellington and His Orchestra. ∾

10

FINALE— THE LAST TOUR

*I*n 1970, Duke was going on 71 years old and had been performing music for over 50 years. He still loved to travel. He loved the anonymity of hotel rooms; he liked room service and being treated like royalty. But he actually kept up this touring to keep the band working. Their payroll was expensive, and bookings were still a night here, a night there. By this time, the turnover in the band was usually due to sad circumstances; Duke outlived several of his musicians, and his long-timers— Johnny Hodges, Cootie Williams, and Lawrence Brown—suffered illnesses and hospitalizations. Hodges died suddenly in 1970; his warm sound on alto saxophone had been the heart of the band's sound.

Even so, beginning in 1970, Duke and the band went on their longest tours ever, to parts of the world they had never set foot in before. They went to the Far East again, and on this trip played concerts in the Philippines, Hong Kong, Singapore, Thailand, Burma, Australia, and New Zealand. The following year, they set off for a five-week State Department tour of what was then the Soviet Union. From there, the band toured Europe for another four weeks then went directly to South America, where they performed in Brazil, Argentina, and Panama for the first time. In 1971, the band logged over 20,000 miles in 12 months—extreme by anyone's standards, not to mention by a bandleader now 72 years old. The jazz journalist Stanley Dance, who frequently traveled with them, documented the band's last years: "After nearly five weeks in Europe, east and west of the Iron Curtain, usually playing

Duke composing on the road, 1967.
Institute of Jazz Studies

two concerts a night—always in a different city and often in a different country—the band left Barcelona for Rio de Janeiro and a month in Latin America. One could only marvel anew at the endurance of the leader, his son, and his musicians."

The United Nations sponsored the performance of the *Third Sacred Concert* at Westminster Abbey in London on October 24, 1973. The concert had a tremendous reception, and the great cathedral was filled. By this time, Duke was carrying all the weight of the band on his shoulders. He had outlived most of his musicians, and dear friends and other former colleagues were passing away. He often appeared exhausted, and needed more rest while traveling than he had previously. Like Billy Strayhorn, Duke was a lifelong smoker, and after several months of hiding his pain, he was diagnosed with lung cancer and lymphoma. He hid these conditions from his musicians, and even from his son Mercer, for as long as he could.

In March 1974, Duke was hospitalized at the Harkness Pavillion of Columbia Presbyterian Hospital, not all that far from his last

"In place of one-nighters in American towns and cities, we now play one-nighters in the cities of different countries. One night we may play Paris, the next Montreal."

Concert program in Burmese for Ellington and His Orchestra's return to Rangoon, Burma (now known as Yangon, Myanmar), Far East Tour, 1972.
Courtesy Morris Hodara

apartment in New York City. He kept a small electric piano at his side, and kept composing. On April 29, Duke's 75th birthday, selections from the *Third Sacred Concert* were performed at the Central Presbyterian Church in New York City, but he was too ill to go.

On May 24, 1974, Duke Ellington died. His funeral was held at the Cathedral of St. John the Divine, the site of Duke's *Second Sacred Concert* and the largest Gothic-style cathedral in the United States. A crowd of over 10,000 people flocked to his funeral. It was a fitting departure for this larger-than-life human being. Generations of musicians were in attendance, including many of Duke's peers: Ella Fitzgerald sang, Count Basie wept.

Duke at the piano, late 1960s.
Photo by Don Hunstein; courtesy Don Hunstein and SONY/BMG Archives

AWARDS AND HONORS

During the course of his long career, Ellington was showered with many honors, in America and abroad. He and several of his top musicians placed high in annual jazz polls from the 1930s on, and Duke himself received 11 Grammy Awards for various recordings. He was given the keys to many cities in the United States and abroad, including New York City, Chicago, and Washington, D.C. He was the recipient of several awards from the NAACP and other civil rights and humanitarian organizations. He was awarded 19 honorary doctorates from colleges and universities all over the country, including Columbia, Yale, Brown, and Howard University. In 1965, he was awarded the President's Gold Medal under Lyndon B. Johnson, and four years later was given the Presidential Medal of Freedom, the highest civilian award granted by the United States, by President Richard M. Nixon. In fact, there are over 300 mayoral proclamations, medals, institutional awards, and international honors that Duke Ellington received in his lifetime.

Yet there was one award not given Duke in his lifetime—the Pulitzer Prize in Music, which is awarded every year to an American composer. In 1965,

the three members of the Pulitzer's music jury recommended Ellington for this special prize, but their recommendation was rejected by the organization's 14-member advisory board. Two of the jury members resigned in protest, and the story made newspaper headlines across the country. Many people felt that the board was demonstrating a prejudice against the African American musical traditions that Duke's music expressed. Duke, in a well-published response to the matter, said simply, "Fate is being kind to me. Fate doesn't want me to be too famous too young." He was hurt, but did not want this incident to destroy his own sense of his musical integrity. Duke received a huge outpouring of support, within the musical world and well beyond it.

Finally, in 1999, tied in with many celebrations of the centennial year of his birth, Edward Kennedy "Duke" Ellington was posthumously awarded a Pulitzer Prize for his great contributions to American music.

Duke receives an honorary doctorate from Columbia University, 1973. Institute of Jazz Studies

THE LEGACY OF DUKE ELLINGTON

Ellington's life work continued after his death. His son Mercer, who had been the band's manager since 1964, fulfilled a commitment Duke had made for a concert in Bermuda the day after his father's funeral. He knew that was what Duke would have wanted. Mercer kept the band going until the late 1980s (Mercer died in 1996), though by then all the longtime Ellington band members had passed away themselves, and the band was largely a new generation of musicians.

Mercer Ellington left an important legacy himself. He restored the band's huge library of scores and parts and helped put together *Sophisticated Ladies,* a long-running Broadway show of Ellington's popular songs. He also put the final touches on *Queenie Pie*, a comic opera Duke had almost finished. Duke would have been thrilled to see the production, which had a month-long run at the Kennedy Center in Washington, D.C. in 1986. In 1988, Mercer arranged for the Smithsonian Institution to acquire Duke Ellington's personal collection of hundreds of original musical scores, notebooks, diaries, photographs, awards, and memorabilia. The Duke Ellington Collection is housed in Washington, D.C., Duke's hometown, in the Archives Center of the National Museum of American History, one of the Smithsonian Museums. It is a unique treasure trove, documenting the achievements and times of an extraordinary man.

Duke Ellington's name and image crop up in everyday places. In 1986, the U.S. Postal

Commemorative U.S. postage stamp, 1986.
Institute of Jazz Studies

Duke Ellington 22 USA

Service issued a commemorative stamp in his honor. The Duke Ellington School of the Arts is a prestigious arts magnet school in Washington D.C. Other schools and streets have been named for him, and a huge statue was built in his honor at the northern corner of Central Park in New York City.

Duke's contributions as a unique musician and composer are discovered and rediscovered by people of all ages, and all across the performing arts. His many compositions and songs offer us new ways to hear things and find inspiration. Many young musicians experience Duke Ellington's legacy in a direct way, by performing it. The Essentially Ellington High School Jazz Band Competition, founded by the Jazz at Lincoln Center organization in 1995, is much more than a jazz contest for

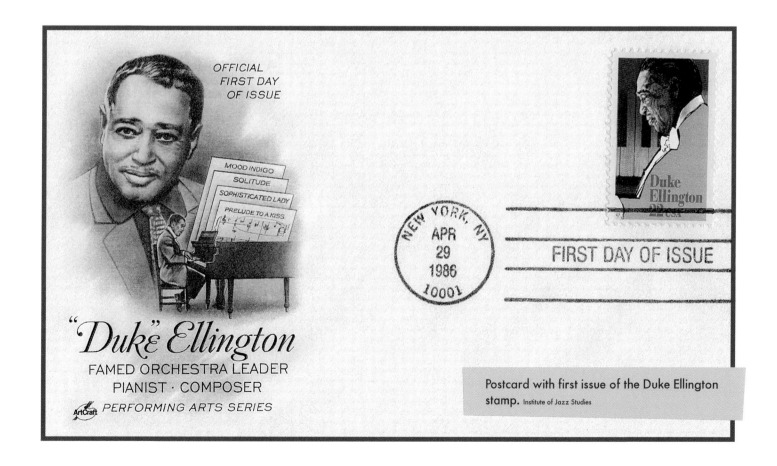

Postcard with first issue of the Duke Ellington stamp. Institute of Jazz Studies

DUKE ELLINGTON'S GREATEST HITS

"Black and Tan Fantasy"

"C-Jam Blues"

"Creole Love Call"

"Do Nothing 'Til You Hear from Me"

"Don't Get Around Much Anymore"

"Drop Me Off in Harlem"

"I Ain't Got Nothin' but the Blues"

"I Got It Bad and That Ain't Good"

"I Let a Song Go Out of My Heart"

"I'm Beginning to See the Light"

"I'm Just a Lucky So-and-So"

"In a Sentimental Mood"

"In My Solitude"

"It Don't Mean a Thing (If It Ain't Got That Swing)"

"Jump for Joy"

"Jungle Nights in Harlem"

"Just a Sittin' and Rockin'"

"Mood Indigo"

"Rockin' in Rhythm"

"Prelude to a Kiss"

"Satin Doll" (Billy Strayhorn)

"Solitude"

"Sophisticated Lady"

"Take the 'A' Train" (Billy Strayhorn)

"Things Ain't What They Used to Be" (Mercer Ellington)

Compositions and Suites

A Drum Is a Woman

Afro-Eurasian Eclipse

Anatomy of a Murder (film score)

Black, Brown and Beige

Creole Rhapsody

Deep South Suite

Far East Suite

Harlem

Jump for Joy (revue)

Liberian Suite

New Orleans Suite

Paris Blues (film score)

The River (ballet)

The Sacred Concerts

Symphony in Black (film score)

teens. By participating, high school jazz bands are given an Ellington curriculum, complete with scores, recordings, and coaches for the finalists. The program focuses on particular tunes and arrangements, and also on the way Duke's musicians developed their unique, individual sounds. To date, more than 200,000 students have performed Duke's music thanks to this program.

"Jazz is many things to many people. To me, it has been a banner under which I have written and played most of life, almost all the way around the world."

Additionally, Duke's music is taught at conservatories and jazz studies classes across the country. The composer Paul Seiko Chihara, who teaches at UCLA, tells his students that Duke Ellington is "our American

Mozart because his music reaches across barriers of classical and popular, concert and saloon, white and black, jazz and classical, male and female—it reaches across all those borders and touches humanity." Beyond category, Duke's music expresses the work of an American master, telling an American story that touches people the world around. Sonny Greer, Duke's drummer from his earliest days as a bandleader said: "Every tick of the clock, somebody in the world is playing an Ellington tune." ∾

Another great recording session, 1959.
Photo by Don Hunstein; courtesy Don Hunstein and SONY/BMG Archives

RESOURCES

SELECTED BIBLIOGRAPHY AND FURTHER READING

FICTION

Curtis, Christopher Paul. *Bud, Not Buddy.* New York: Random House Children's Books, 2004.

Myers, Walter Dean. *Harlem Summer.* New York: Scholastic Press, 2007.

Tate, Eleanora. *Celeste's Harlem Renaissance.* New York: Little, Brown & Co., 2007.

NONFICTION

Armstrong, Louis. *In His Own Words: Selected Writings.* 2nd rev. ed. New York: Oxford University Press, 2001.

Bankston, John. *The Life and Times of Duke Ellington* (Masters of Music). Mitchell Lane Publishers, 2004.

Dance, Stanley. *The World of Duke Ellington.* New York: Scribner's, 1970. Reprint, New York: Da Capo, 1981.

Ellington, Duke. *Music Is My Mistress.* Garden City, NY: Doubleday, 1973. Reprint, New York: Da Capo, 1976.

Frankl, Ron. *Duke Ellington.* New York: Chelsea House, 1988.

Giddins, Gary. *Satchmo: The Genius of Louis Armstrong.* 2nd rev. ed. New York: Da Capo Press, 2001.

Gutman, Bill. *Duke Ellington.* New York: Random House, 1977.

Handy, W.C. *Father of the Blues, an Autobiography.* New York: The Macmillan Company, 1941.

Hardy, Stephen P. *Extraordinary People of the Harlem Renaissance.* New York: Children's Press, 2000.

Hasse, John Edward. *Beyond Category: The Life and Genius of Duke Ellington.* New York: Simon & Schuster, 1993.

Hill, Laban Carrick. *Harlem Stomp! A Cultural History of the Harlem Renaissance.* New York: Little, Brown & Co., 2003.

Marvin, Martin. *Extraordinary People in Jazz.* New York: Children's Press, 2004.

Monceaux, Morgan. *Jazz: My Music, My People.* New York: Knopf Books for Young Readers, 1994.

Tucker, Mark. *Ellington: The Early Years.* Urbana: University of Illinois Press, 1991.

Vail, Ken. *Duke's Diary: The Life of Duke Ellington, Parts One and Two.* Lanham, MD: Scarecrow Press, Inc. and Oxford, 2002.

Waldo, Terry. *This Is Ragtime.* New York: Da Capo Press, Inc. 1991 (paperback ed.) 1976.

RECOMMENDED RECORDINGS, FILMS, AND WEB SITES

There are many reissued recordings available by Duke Ellington and His Orchestra by record labels whose ownership has changed. Some recordings are now available in new CD collections; the same is true of DVD versions of Duke Ellington's film appearances and soundies. Additionally, Web sites and their titles are subject to change; however, the Web sites of the national organizations included here are well established and generally keep their links and respective resource listings up to date.

RECORDINGS

And His Mother Called Him Bill (A Tribute to Billy Strayhorn)

The Best of the Duke Ellington Centennial Edition (1 CD)

The Centennial Edition—Highlights from 1927–1973 (3-CD set)

Ella Fitzgerald Sings the Duke Ellington Song Book

Ellington at Newport, 1956

The Essential Duke Ellington (2-CD set)

The Far East Suite

The Queen's Suite

Such Sweet Thunder

Three Suites (includes the Ellington Nutcracker)

The Very Best of Duke Ellington, RCA Victor

FILMS

Black and Tan, 1929 (19 minutes)

A Bundle of Blues, 1933 (9 minutes)

Belle of the Nineties, 1934 (featuring
   Mae West)
Symphony in Black, 1934 (9 minutes)
Hot Chocolate, Jam Session, 1941 soundies
Cabin in the Sky, 1942
Reveille with Beverly, 1942
Anatomy of a Murder, 1959
   (Ellington wrote the score, and appears
   briefly)
Paris Blues, 1961 (Ellington wrote
   the score)
Concert of Sacred Music, 1965
On the Road with Duke Ellington, 1967

Web Sites

America's Story, from America's Library
www.americaslibrary.gov
An interesting site for students from the Library of Congress in Washington, D.C., the largest library in the world. Duke Ellington and other pioneering American musicians are featured in the site's *Meet Amazing Americans* section.

Billy Strayhorn—A Legend in Jazz
www.billystrayhorn.com
A comprehensive and elegantly designed site devoted to the life and music of Billy Strayhorn, Ellington's longtime collaborator.

Duke Ellington: Celebrating 100 Years of the Man and His Music
www.dellington.org
This online exhibition is a collaborative production by the National Museum of American History, the Music Educator's National Conference (MENC), and the Kennedy Center/ArtsEdge. Includes a time line, interactive scrapbook, a student gallery of work inspired by Ellington, and more.

Duke Ellington: "The Maestro"
www.npr.org/templates/story/story.php?
   storyId=16054497
A four-part radio series devoted to Duke Ellington that was broadcast on National Public Radio in the fall of 2007, available for listening and downloads.

The Duke Ellington Collection, National Museum of American History
http://americanhistory.si.edu/archives/
   d5301.htm
The *Duke Ellington Collection, 1927–1988* is one of the largest collections in *The American Music Collections* at the National Museum of American History (one of the Smithsonian Museums) in Washington, D.C. The bulk of the material is dated from 1934 to 1974 and includes recordings, original music manuscripts, handwritten notes, correspondence,

business records, photographs, scrapbooks, and all kinds of memorabilia. This site shows the scope of the collection, and what is available to view online.

The Duke Ellington Society

http://museum.media.org/duke/essence/
    index_ie.html

This is the official Web site of the Duke Ellington Society in New York City, founded in 1959 and devoted to promoting the appreciation of Ellington through meetings, concerts, a newsletter, and discussion groups. It's a great place for biographical information about Duke Ellington and listings of Ellington events and resources.

Duke Ellington's Washington

www.pbs.org/ellingtonsdc/noteMusicians.
    htm

This PBS site documents the African American community in Washington, D.C. that was home to Duke Ellington in the early 1900s, as well as other prominent African Americans.

JAZZ: A Film by Ken Burns

www.pbs.org/jazz/biography/artist_id_
    ellington_duke.htm

This interactive site based on the PBS television series *Jazz* (produced by Ken Burns) includes biographies of Ellington and other important jazz musicians, with audio samples from different periods of Duke's career.

Jazz for Young People Curriculum

www.jalc.org/jazzED/j4yp_curr/contents
    Page.html

In addition to providing supplementary material for teachers and students at Lincoln Center's Jazz for Young People, this site serves as a comprehensive beginner's guide to jazz history, jazz styles, and important jazz musicians.

Jazz in America

www.jazzinamerica.org/home.asp

The Web site of *The Thelonious Monk Institute of Jazz*. Includes the Institute's online jazz curricula for three grade levels, jazz resources, and news and information about Institute activities.

William P. Gottlieb: Photographs from the Golden Age of Jazz

http://memory.loc.gov/ammem/wghtml/
    wghome.html

This online Library of Congress American Memory collection showcases the work of jazz photographer William P. Gottlieb. It presents some of Gottlieb's most famous photographs from between 1938 and 1948, including many of Duke Ellington, annotated contact prints, and related magazine articles.

INDEX

Photos are denoted by **bold type**